I dedicate this book to three women who have been a huge part of not just this book but every book of mine. They put so much time and effort into making these books magical; they are the unseen heroes.

Clare Marshall, for your vision, support and guidance, and for being the world's best editor. You always notice the magic of each book, and you take so much care to create something we are all so proud of.

Designer Michelle Mackintosh, I know how much time and thought you put into every single moment of each book; your planning starts a year out. You are wonderfully whimsical to work with and very inspiring.

And finally, Armelle Habib. You are one of the most humble, honest and down-to-earth photographers I have ever known. I feel so safe working with you and always trust your eye. It is an absolute honour to have worked with you on this book and this very raw, real and honest cover.

To these three remarkable women, I cannot thank you enough for working so hard to turn our dream into a reality.

Recipes and remedies for radiant skin, eyes, hair and nails

LOLA BERRY'S

BEAUTY FOOD

plum.

Pan Macmillan Australia

CONTENTS

INTRODUCTION 7

Introduction

This book is about helping you nourish yourself from the inside, which reflects on the outside. I think healthy people look unreal – you want to know what their magic secret is, which is often just a case of them really looking after themselves and caring about how they nurture their body, mind and spirit. When it comes to health, it's all about the big picture, looking after *all* elements of your health.

The truth is, I look at other girls and think, 'Oh wow, she's stunning, I wish I looked like her.' Every year when the spectacular Victoria's Secret show rolls around I find myself going on a detox and vowing to get that perfect body, those amazing long locks, that perfect complexion. But you know what? I'm fighting a losing battle, because I can't be them (not to mention I'm only 5'3, so good luck, Lols), just like you can't be them, and I can't be you, and you can't be me. We really only have one option, which is to simply be ourselves. I think we often spend a big hunk of time trying to be something we're not or hiding who we really are. But the moment you embrace who you are, well, that's when you'll find yourself at your most sparkly and beautiful.

There's this awesome word in yoga – santosha – which is all about being cool with the uncool. I loved this concept immediately when I heard it in class, because I was moving house and so stressed out by it all. But when I sat with this idea of santosha, I realised it's about loving yourself whole, learning to love the little imperfections (becoming content with who you are), the things you want to change and knowing that they are in fact the things that make you perfectly you. When we come to that place of loving who we are, the next steps become a whole lot of fun: if you want to try beauty-inspired recipes because you want to feel your best and, in turn, glow from the inside out, you're not doing it because you want to look like a cover girl or impress a boy. At the end of the day, the only person you need to worry about impressing is you.

I am here to tell you that I firmly believe that what you eat impacts on the way you look and ultimately the way in which you age. These recipes (both topical and for eating) will help to make you look your best. What we eat has a huge impact on how firm and smooth our skin is and how clear the whites of our eyes are. Ageing is, in part, caused by free radical damage (the sun is a contributor to this, too), but by increasing the amount of antioxidants we eat and decreasing the foods that cause inflammation and free radical damage we can really help to slow down the ageing process and start to glow. I know when I really look after my diet, I look vibrant and fresh. When I'm not eating properly or the sugary foods start creeping in, my complexion turns grey and I look older and more tired. So let's do everything in our power to help ourselves not only feel our best but look it, too – bring on that natural dewy glow!

ONE

THE
BEAUTY
LOWDOWN

ALL THE TIPS AND TRICKS YOU NEED TO KNOW

Anti-ageing tips and tricks

Anybody who knows me knows that I love to live like a mermaid.
Having lived on the Gold Coast, I've had my fair share of sun exposure
(and, to be honest, probably a little too much of it at times).

Since turning 30, I'm all about ageing gracefully. I've tried a fair few anti-ageing tricks, from face masks and peels, to microdermabrasions and jade rollers on my face. But the simple truth is that these things can cost a bucket-load of money and there are so many other things we can do without taking out a loan from the bank. First up, if you want to focus on anti-ageing, it starts with diet. When I meet someone new, I always notice in their face (no matter how old they are) if they are vital or not. I believe this comes down to diet and how you choose to look after yourself. Someone that truly nourishes themselves will have a glow, and they will also age gracefully. The good news is that this entire book is designed to help you eat in a way that nourishes you from the inside out.

Next up is sun protection. Yes, the sun ages you, so when you go walking or head off to the beach for the day, be prepared and take a good hat, sunnies and a strong sunscreen (I like 30–50 plus). Now, I know the next question is going to be, 'What about all the chemicals in the sunscreen?'. Well, there are some amazing natural and organic options out there and although it is trial and error to find the right fit for you (as they tend to have different consistencies), good ones do exist.

My last tip for anti-ageing is to remember to protect your neck, décolletage and the backs of your hands, as they will often give away your age before your face does. I treat the backs of my hands as I do my face. Any time I put a face mask or sunscreen on, I also pop a bit onto my hands – it's become part of my daily ritual. Try leaving some sunscreen in your car so you can apply each morning before driving, or just keep it in your handbag.

All things hydration

✦

Hydration is king when it comes to health, and if you take one thing from this book, I would say: up your water consumption. We are dehydrated more often than not – and do you know what the first sign of dehydration is? Hunger. We think we should eat something, when in actual fact, we probably just need a good old gulp of water. As a nutritionist, I always told my clients to aim to drink about 1 litre of water per 22 kg of body weight per day. That sounds like heaps, I know, and you're probably thinking 'Yeah right, Lols, I'll be dashing to the loo every 5 minutes!' Well, you will be if you increase your water intake drastically, so the trick is to increase it very slowly.

- **Filtered vs tap** If you have access to great filtered water that's brilliant, but don't let the fact that you may only have access to tap water stop you from getting in some sweet-as hydration.

- **Plastic bottles** I do think too much plastic is a no-go and the plastic can leach chemicals into the water, especially when it's been exposed to too much sunlight or heat. If I'm drinking out of a plastic bottle – which I sometimes do when I'm on the run – and I accidentally leave it in my car, I always throw it out.

- **Glass vs BPA-free vs copper** There are so many different schools of thought when it comes to what we should be drinking our water out of. I do love a good bottle; glass is great but can be heavy and no fun when it smashes on the ground – I've been there once or twice – and although the BPA-free plastic bottles are often nice and sturdy, some people are still funny about them, so you've got to do your research. Then there's my new thing: copper bottles. In ayurvedic medicine, drinking out of copper is said to balance your doshas (that's kapha, vata and pitta) and aid digestion. Plus, I kind of like the taste! Copper is known to scientists and the medical community as having antibacterial, antimicrobial, antiviral and anti-inflammatory properties, which can help to speed up recovery times and heal wounds. It's also said to boost our immune systems and help keep our skin glowing, so you can see why I'm sold. Oh, and I forgot to mention that they are also very pretty.

Sleep: the miracle youth elixir

✱

I like to call sleep the wonder-drug. The truth is, when you're not getting enough shut-eye you'll know about it, and it will show on your face. For me, it's much more than that, though. When I don't sleep properly I start to crave sugars, and when sugars creep into my diet, that's when my complexion turns grey and I feel like I lose that fresh glow. So for me, it's a two-pronged effect.

Now there's sleep and then there's *sleep*. We need REM (Rapid Eye Movement) sleep to help repair the body, as this is when the body becomes temporarily paralysed and healing occurs. We're meant to go through cycles of five stages of sleep each night, so a good night's sleep can mean you get to experience REM sleep four or fives times per night! So, the earlier you get to bed and the longer you spend there the better. Most of us thrive off a solid eight hours, and it's said that every hour you sleep before midnight is the equivalent to two hours after midnight. I have a little ritual that helps me to fall asleep, because I often find myself stressing out and going over things in my mind rather than calming down and getting some solid shut-eye. And even though I travel heaps, I have learned to take these habits with me wherever I go.

- **6–7 pm dinner** This might seem early, but ideally you want three hours post dinner to let it digest, so that when you're sleeping, your body is focusing on recharging and healing, as opposed to digesting your last meal. I definitely notice that I don't sleep well if I've eaten too late at night.

- **8 pm digestion tea or sleepy-time tea** At this point, I drink a store-bought tea that is often a gentle combination of herbs with calming properties. While I'm having this tea I'll often do a last email check for the day.

- **8:30 pm candles and calming music** I love to use music to help get me into a calm state. Recently, I have been listening to movie scores and classical music – my current favourite is Ludovico Einaudi – but I also love Nicolas Jaar, Jónsi, Sigur Ròs, Oliver Tank, The National, Bing & Ruth, Bon Iver, Jack Grace and Bonobo. I'm quite the musical nerd – in fact, when I teach yoga I will set the music before I plan the actual yoga poses.

- **9 pm in bed** At this point I try to be in bed with a book and my tunes on, or sometimes I do love to zone out by finding something to watch on Netflix. My advice is to do whatever feels like you're giving back to yourself and creating your own little sanctuary. I will still check my phone while I'm watching something, but I switch the screen to night-time mode so the blue light doesn't over-stimulate me and make me stay awake.

- **9:30–10 pm sleep** This is when I try to nod off to sleep. I pop a few drops of a sleepy oil blend on my pillow, put my favourite crystal underneath and drift off.

One more note on skin, hair and sleep: I also use a silk pillowcase, which I know sounds silly, but when I was travelling in America the girls who did my hair said it would make my blow wave last longer, and sure enough it does. It's said to be great for your skin, too, reducing the morning 'creases' that can be visible after sleeping on a regular pillowcase and helping to reduce redness and puffiness. Silk also has a cooling effect, so can help prevent you from sweating too much in the night. If you have long hair, you'll know that this can be seriously annoying. So, for soft skin and a longer-lasting blow wave I'm all for the silk pillowcase! Try looking for them at Target, Big W, Myer, Kmart, David Jones – trust me, they're easy to find.

Shopping for cosmetics and skin care

What chemicals, ingredients and products should you avoid? This can be so confusing, and I always have to research what to stay away from, what's a maybe and what is safe and therefore okay to put on my skin. So, this is my stay-away-from list, mainly because they're toxic and harmful to our bodies.

- **Sodium Laureth Sulphate (SLS)** This foaming agent is one of the first bad chemicals I learned about when I was younger, when my mum took me to a talk about natural skin care. It's said to mimic the effects of oestrogen and has been linked to being a skin irritant and carcinogen.

- **Propylene Glycol/Polyethylene Glycol (PEG)** This is the stuff people refer to when they say anti-freeze is in skin products. It's said to have bad effects on major organs like the liver, kidneys and even the brain. So, no dice from me.

- **Parabens** These are used as preservatives in skin products and are no good, as their use has been linked to increased risk of breast cancer.

- **Phthalates** These guys are used in loads of things. They are referred to as plasticisers, as they help to give products a plastic-like texture – they're kind of like a synthetic resin. Phthalates are linked to low sperm counts, birth defects and may increase the risk of cancers.

- **Siloxanes** These are used to soothe skin but they are said to mess with our hormones.

- **Sodium Borate (also Boric Acid)** This is used in hand soaps and laundry powders and has been banned in a few countries, so we know it's got to go eventually. It's said that regular exposure affects male fertility by potentially causing a lower sperm count.

- **Petroleum-based products or petroleum byproducts** These not only clog the pores but have been said to have a carcinogenic effect on the body.

- **Formaldehyde** I was taught at uni that this is what's used as embalming fluid. It's mainly found in products like nail polish and it's known to be carcinogenic, plus it's an allergen and an irritant.

- **Deodorant** This is one product I only use natural versions of; I'm not down with aluminium and chemicals being applied that close to my lymph glands.

My morning and night face rituals

* **AM** I'm usually in a mega-rush, so I'll quickly splash water on my face, then cleanse, tone and moisturise. I also pop a few dabs of eye cream on, then mascara and eyeliner (I use organic and natural products for a chilled day of meetings, then the real McCoy for shoots).

* **PM** Twice a week I apply some kind of face mask (any of the ones from this book; I do try to rotate and mix it up so my skin is getting different forms of nourishment). First of all, I use a make-up wipe and remove any make-up I have on, then with clean, dry hands I apply the mask and leave it on for around 10 minutes. I usually wash it off in the shower, where I'll also cleanse my face, neck and décolletage. When I get out, I tone and often put oils and serums on. I look pretty shiny when I go to bed, but I love knowing they have all night to work their magic. Usually by the time I wake up my skin has absorbed all the goodness.

How to shop for natural beauty – what to look out for

What's good and what's marketing? Even I get confused and it's really more about becoming a detective. First up, there are a few things I look for: not tested on animals, inclusion of natural ingredients and exclusion of the nasties (see page 18). I look at the ingredient list and figure out how many ingredients I understand and I'll often do a quick google if I'm not sure, then I'll try it on the back of my hand to see how it feels for a few minutes. If I'm still not sure, I ask questions: it's kind of like being at the farmers' market and asking what they use on their crops if they don't have organic certification.

A word on palm oil and orangutans

This is a passion of mine – that the mass slaughter of orangutans that's occurring just to provide us with palm oil comes to a stop. Know this: you get to vote with your dollar and each and every one of you can make a change, so please feel empowered to support brands and products whose values are in line with your own.

Here are a few facts (head to **www.orangutan.org.au** to find out more):

• Palm oil is used in everything from snack foods to soaps. It is found in more than half of all packaged items on our supermarket shelves.

• Every hour, 300 football fields of precious remaining forest are ploughed to the ground across South-East Asia to make way for palm oil plantations.

• In the last 20 years, more than 3.5 million hectares of Indonesian and Malaysian forest have been destroyed to make way for palm oil plantations.

• Almost 80 per cent of orangutan habitat has disappeared in the last 20 years.

• We are losing more than 6,000 orangutans a year.

What to do? Well, first of all let's support products that are either palm oil–free or made with sustainably and ethically produced oils. Also know that palm oil isn't just used in skin care, it's in about 300 supermarket products – think cookies, chocolate bars, ice cream, crackers, cereals, doughnuts, potato chips, even instant noodles – so read the labels and know that it can be listed as vegetable oil, so it's worth becoming a bit of a detective to figure out which brands you want to support. You can totally make a difference, always remember that.

Travel tips

I'm not going to sugar-coat it for you, looking after your face, eyes, skin, hair and nails takes work, but if you make it non-negotiable then you can take it with you everywhere, much like your health. You can be healthy anywhere in the world and unhealthy anywhere in the world. Simply put, being healthy is making the choice to put yourself first, so choose it for you because you love and value yourself.

Here are my tips for when I travel:

- **Pack a kit** No matter where I'm going I always have my little kit of face cleanser, toner and moisturiser, and I apply these not just to my face and neck but also my décolletage and hands. If you're worried about the size of your bottles, buy travel-sized containers from the chemist and tip your products into them.

- **Take face masks when you travel** I buy the single-sheet masks so I can use them and not worry about repacking or things spilling. I have recently found single-use hand and foot masks, too; they're a lot of fun and your skin feels so smooth afterwards.

- **Toner mists for flying** I buy these in travel size and love spritzing mid-flight. They not only smell great but keep you feeling fresh and hydrated. On a long-haul flight, I will use a toner mist and then moisturise my hands, arms and face multiple times. I notice my skin dries out loads when I fly so I do this every few hours. A good trick is to check and reapply between movies!

- **Water is key, so keep sipping away** I also pack my own tea bags, as I like to drink detox tea blends and nettle tea to help with flushing out toxins while flying.

- **Food** This is a tricky one; I've travelled and just tried to make the best of what's available and I've travelled with my own stuff packed, and I can tell you I bounce back so much faster when I take my own food. When I eat plane food I feel like the jetlag lasts longer and I feel bloated for about three days. I can't stand that feeling so I simply pack my own now. I'll take a salad and a protein for the first leg of the flight (often it's simply leftover dinner from the night before), then snacks such as raw trail mix. I also pack the healthiest protein bars I can find, make energy balls and take chopped veggie sticks with hummus. In addition, I pack greens powders and mix them with water. It can get a little messy but I love knowing I can bring my health with me wherever I go.

- **Sleep** I don't take any kind of sleeping tablets, as I don't like the idea of how they make you feel afterwards. I'm a little bit of a hippie about that kind of thing, but I do believe you've got to make it work for you. I would advise to stay off the booze on long-haul flights as it will only dehydrate you further and compound your jetlag, not to mention the effect on your skin. Personally, I just grab whatever sleep I can knowing that if I stay healthy on the flight it will be easier to catch up on sleep when I arrive and let my body clock adjust to the new surroundings.

- **Grounding** Whenever I land somewhere new, especially if it's overseas, I will make sure I find some kind of Mother Nature and take my shoes off and ground myself. Some people call this 'earthing' but basically you want to whip your shoes off and let the earth centre and connect you. I have recently learned a new word which I love almost as much as 'biophilia' (the healing power of connecting with Mother Nature). It's called 'nelipot' and it means a person who walks without shoes or chooses to go barefoot. This will ground you straight away. The chiropractor I used to see for years would always tell me to walk around barefoot as much as possible, so I really love embracing this whimsical 'nelipot' way of living whenever I can. When I visit my agent's office, I'll often wear heels in and then whip them straight off for the actual meeting to feel more grounded, connected and focused. And yes, as I write this book I am most certainly embracing the 'nelipot' life!

A sugar Q&A
with David Gillespie

❋

David Gillespie is the author of the bestselling *Sweet Poison* books, exposing the links between sugar and obesity, as well *Toxic Oil, Free Schools, Big Fat Lies* and the *Eat Real Food* books. He's also a dead-set legend, and kindly offered to answer some sugar-related questions for me!

How do we slow down the ageing process with our diet?

Don't eat sugar. You will still age, of course, but it will just be a lot slower. Sugar interferes with collagen – that's the thing that keeps our skin elastic. The more sugar you eat, the more elasticity you lose, thus speeding up the ageing process. Sugar is made up of both fructose and glucose, and it's the fructose component that does all the damage. Fructose effectively ages us at ten times the rate that glucose does. Cutting out sugar will be much more effective and cheaper than smearing some sort of cream all over your face!

Where is sugar mainly hidden when it comes to everyday foods?

When we think about sugar, we think about chocolate bars and lollies. While these ones are the obvious culprits, it's often things that are branded as healthy that contain hidden sugar. Brekkie cereals are often full of sugar! Thirty per cent of your average breakfast cereal is sugar. Juices are another biggie. Also watch out for sauces, dips and condiments, which are often a quick way to add a couple of teaspoons of sugar to your diet without realising it. Even muesli and granola bars can be full of sugar.

Does sugar cause inflammation in the body?

Yes it does. It's definitely not a good idea to be having it in your diet. When there's inflammation in the body, there is more free radical damage, which isn't going to help with wrinkles.

Do you have a favourite youth elixir food?

Eggs will do it. They're a very complete and whole food, containing both complete protein and good fats, plus a nice hit of vitamins and minerals. You could survive on eggs and just the occasional bit of veggie or fruit for vitamin C.

Yoga for beauty

✳

When you hear people say that they've got that yoga glow, it's because yoga poses work on helping you glow from the inside out. Much like nourishing yourself with food, yoga works on your internal organs and stimulates the flow of energy, prana or qi (whatever you prefer to call it). So, if you want that glowing complexion, then yoga is the go-to exercise in my book.

Forearm wheel
(Dwi Pada Viparita
Dandasana)

Here are a few poses to get you started that are great for beauty and helping you glow:

- **Forearm wheel (Dwi Pada Viparita Dandasana)** This pose is a progression from wheel pose, so make sure you're feeling good in wheel before giving this one a crack – though I will say, for me this pose sometimes feels easier than the traditional wheel. I get into this pose by doing a full wheel, then cradling my head coming down onto my forearms, giving me a deeper opening of my heart space, chest and shoulders. This pose will energise you and open your heart, so you'll be super glowing and putting the very best version of yourself forward. It's my secret pre-date weapon!

- **Chair pose (Utkatasana)** This is a deep squat pose that challenges the body and therefore forces the heart rate to accelerate, increasing circulation and inducing sweat by building heat within the body. It's this sweat that helps us to get rid of any impurities. In yoga it's referred to as 'tapas' or a fire within the body and mind. This pose is also seen as being good for mental discipline and is great for getting focused.

- **Plough pose (Halasana)** In this pose your feet are lifted over your head and ideally pressed into the ground (although it can take some time to get your feet to touch the ground, so don't rush it). I personally get into this pose from a continuation of the shoulder stand. Blood flow rushes towards your face, which again helps with a healthy, glowing complexion.

- **Seated twist (Ardha Matsyendrasana)** Any twisting pose will help the body to detoxify, as it works on stimulating the organs of elimination. I always make sure I engage 'Uddiyana Bandha', which means my core is turned on (suck your navel towards your spine) to protect my lower back whenever I twist. Also, after you've done a lot of twisting postures like this one, make sure you drink plenty of water to help flush out toxins. I always notice if I've had a few drinks the night before a yoga class, as I can smell the alcohol in my sweat. It sounds gross but at least you know it's come out, which I love. This pose will aid digestion, too.

- **Forward fold (Uttanasana)** This is technically a gentle inversion: a forward-bending pose that forces new blood flow into the face fast, bringing with it oxygen and other helpful nutrients that fight free radicals, encourage skin-cell renewal and help give your face that rosy, dewy glow. Don't worry about touching your toes, it's more about relaxing and letting gravity work its magic.

- **Camel pose (Ustrasana)** This deep backward bend is an advanced pose, so take it slowly and listen to your body. If you haven't tried it before, starting on your knees and leaning back is fine. The intense back bend helps to open up the heart space and rib cage, increasing lung capacity for inhaling more oxygen, reducing stress and balancing the hormones in the body that are responsible for acne and pimple outbursts. It's also said to be yoga's antidepressant pose, as it lifts your mood and helps you to let go of sadness, especially that associated with heartbreak. Take it from me first-hand, it really does have an impact.

- **Fish pose (Matsyasana)** This pose is said to help with your complexion. As you arch your head and neck backwards, blood will flow to the face. Take three to six rounds of lion's breath here, too, to further eliminate toxins from the body – inhaling through your nose and exhaling with your mouth open wide and your tongue sticking out. It sounds and looks weird but works wonders.

Chair pose
(Utkatasana)

Plough pose
(Halasana)

Seated twist
(Ardha Matsyendrasana)

Forward fold
(Uttanasana)

Camel pose
(Ustrasana)

Fish pose
(Matsyasana)

Cook's notes

✤

Notes on the recipes

- Cooking temperatures are for a regular or conventional oven. If you are using a fan-forced oven, you'll need to drop the cooking temperature by 10–20°C (check your oven manual).

- Wherever possible, all the foods I eat and use in my recipes are whole, raw, organic, seasonal, unprocessed and as close to their natural state as possible. If you can, do the same.

- Assume that any fresh fruits (bananas, mangoes, avocados etc.) are ripe, unless I say otherwise.

The following ingredients appear in lots of my recipes, and I want to share a couple of tips here just in case you're not familiar with their preparation.

Coconut oil is solid at room temperature, so can be tricky to measure. I pop the jar into a pot of hot water to melt the oil.

I always use **activated nuts** in my recipes. This means I soak them in water for 2–3 hours (or overnight if possible) and then rinse. This removes enzyme inhibitors and makes them easier to digest. After rinsing (unless you're about to blend them up for a smoothie or raw treat, when you want that creamy texture), spread the nuts out on a baking tray and place them in a 50°C oven or dehydrator to dry out (this will take anywhere from 6–24 hours depending on the temperature). Store your activated nuts in sealed glass jars in the pantry.

Olive oil in my recipes is almost always extra-virgin (unless I'm deliberately trying to avoid its peppery taste) – this means that it's the first pressing with no chemicals or additives. Regular olive oil becomes unstable and rancid when used in cooking at high temperatures, but good-quality extra-virgin varieties are much higher in polyphenols (the antioxidant part of the olive oil) and this prevents the double bond in the mono-unsaturated fat from breaking when heated.

When I talk about seasoning with **salt** in my recipes, I'm not referring to table salt, which is highly processed. I love to use pink salt – it tastes just like normal salt but has loads more minerals (about 84 trace minerals, in fact). It's great to use in place of regular table salt and looks so pretty. I use Murray River or Himalayan. Celtic salt and rock salt are good options, too. Use salt sparingly, though, and stay away from the bleached stuff.

Instead of soy sauce in my recipes I like to use **tamari** – a Japanese fermented soy sauce with a darker colour and richer flavour than traditional soy sauce. It contains much less salt and is a good source of vitamin B3, protein and manganese. It is also made with far less wheat than normal soy sauce, if any, and is therefore a good low-gluten or gluten-free alternative. Look for gluten free on the label.

When I mention **red chillies** in a recipe, I'm usually referring to the long, thin cayenne chillies that you can get at any supermarket. These are quite mild compared to other varieties, but they are still very spicy. You simply trim the stem and slice them thinly, using the seeds and all. (Make sure you wash your hands after chopping them, and don't get the juice in your eyes.) If you're not big on chillies, use less than I suggest, or if you love them, by all means add more or use the hotter varieties. I'm a big fan of bird's eye chillies, which are very hot!

I like to cook with **oats**, and often use them in my recipes. Although oats themselves don't contain gluten, because of the way we process them, most oatmeal brands have been cross-contaminated with minuscule amounts of wheat, barley and/or rye, so we can't call them 'gluten free'. About 30 per cent of people who have coeliac disease cannot tolerate oats (even when the cross-contamination is almost eliminated), so if you have coeliac disease, or a particularly severe gluten allergy, proceed with caution.

I often use **almond milk** in my recipes as a dairy alternative, but there are heaps of others you could use in its place, such as milk made from oats, rice, cashews, macadamia nuts, quinoa and hazelnuts. It's easy to make your own if you have a really good food processor. The ratio is 1 cup of nuts to 2 cups (500 ml) of water. You'll need to soak them overnight first, and give them a good rinse. Strain through a fine mesh sieve and you're done! (You can save the fibrous bits and use them for a raw treat recipe, or simply add them to a granola mix.) If you don't have time to make your own nut milk, you can buy it off the shelf. Just read the labels and stay away from the stuff with loads of sugars or sweeteners. And watch out for preservatives. There should only be about four ingredients and you should be able to pronounce all of them. If you can't (or they are just numbers), look them up to see if they come from a natural source.

Natural sweeteners are another ingredient in my recipes that you can easily change to suit you. There's coconut nectar, maple syrup, stevia, dates, figs, agave, raw honey, rice malt syrup, coconut palm sugar, rapadura (also called panela), monk fruit extract and yacon syrup – have I forgotten anything? Remember that even natural sweeteners should only be used to slightly sweeten something; they shouldn't be guzzled down just because you bought them from a health-food store (I fell into that trap once – never again). If you can't tolerate too much fructose then you need to be careful with sweeteners such as agave and honey. My advice? Try a little first. Some people don't like the aftertaste of stevia, while I quite enjoy it. It's about trying things out and finding what works best for you. If you feel bloated, grumpy or lethargic after using a particular sweetener, try something else.

TWO

FACE

RECIPES AND REMEDIES

Hero ingredients

When it comes to beauty, we probably spend the most time and money on our faces (and hair). It might be facials or treatments – I've tried all sorts of things, such as peels, microdermabrasion and light therapy, to get that beautiful glow. A lot, however, can be achieved through diet, and each of the recipes in this section has been created to help with collagen production, age prevention, reduction of free radical damage and balancing hormones, which can often cause havoc with our skin. These recipes are my favourites for getting that glowy, youthful look.

Blueberries

We know that blueberries are good for us; they're at the top of any superfoods list because they're full of anti-ageing antioxidants. These antioxidants are now being studied for their powers in helping to prevent Alzheimer's and other degenerative diseases. When it comes to beauty, the antioxidant anthocyanin (a flavonoid) – the stuff that makes blueberries blue – helps to combat free radical damage and protect against inflammation, which is a leading factor in not just skin ageing but also brain ageing.

Chocolate

As if I was going to write a book without a chocolate hero. I probably have the world's biggest sweet tooth! The truth is, chocolate is brilliant for skin health. Dark chocolate (we're talking about 70 per cent cocoa and raw cacao powder) helps combat beauty's number-one enemy: stress. Cacao helps reduce stress, which means less collagen breakdown and therefore less wrinkles. Flavonols (the type of flavonoid found in chocolate) are antioxidants that enable your skin to glow really naturally by helping it protect itself from UV damage, fight free radicals and increase blood flow.

Macadamia nuts

If you want good skin, then you need good fats in your diet, and that's where these guys come in. We're so lucky in Australia, as macadamias are our native nut (they're often referred to as the Queensland nut or Bauple nut, after Mount Bauple). When I lived on the Gold Coast, I used to go to the Byron Bay farmers' market each weekend and drive past all the macadamia fields on the way. I would buy fresh, raw macadamia nut butter, and it became my favourite snack in the whole wide world. As soon as I got home from the market, I'd whip up some gluten-free buckwheat bread, slather it with fresh macadamia nut butter and top it with a thick layer of homemade raspberry jam and some fresh strawberries – it became my Sunday tradition, complete with salty hair from beach swims and bare feet. One thing I always noticed was that my skin was smoother and glowed more when I lived on the Gold Coast, and I put that down to the ocean swims and the high quantities of macadamia nuts and macadamia nut butter in my diet. My skin thrived off the good fats.

Maca powder

First up, I want to warn you that this stuff tastes a bit like burnt marshmallows, but when it's mixed with other ingredients it has a nice, full earthy flavour It's a Peruvian root vegetable known for its hormone-modulating effects, and it's also said to increase libido (especially in males). When we have breakouts around our chin and the lower third of the face, it can be due to hormone imbalances, which is why we often get breakouts right before that time of the month. So maca comes to the rescue by helping to balance out these hormones.

Maca, macadamia and carob shake

*

I love this shake because it feels like a treat. I also like that it uses carob instead of cacao, as it contains no caffeine, so this recipe is a goodie even if you make it at night-time. It's pretty filling though, so I like it for brekkie or as a morning snack!

1 frozen banana (peel it before you freeze it)

2 medjool dates, pitted

1 teaspoon maca powder

pinch of ground nutmeg

pinch of ground cinnamon

1 tablespoon carob powder, plus extra to sprinkle on top

¼ cup (40 g) macadamia nuts, plus extra, crushed, to serve

1–1¼ cups (250–310 ml) macadamia nut milk

Pop everything into a blender and blitz it up, adding a little extra nut milk, if necessary, to reach your desired consistency. Pour into glasses, sprinkle with a little extra carob powder and a few extra crushed macadamia nuts, and serve.

Serves 2

TIPS
You can substitute the dates for 1 tablespoon rice malt syrup or maple syrup. You can use any nut milk for this recipe; I like to use macadamia but almond works really well, too.

Three berry collagen-boosting porridge

❋

I'm a huge porridge fan – it's a great way to set you up with lots of long-lasting energy. This recipe is very low in sugar, too – I find when I add cinnamon to porridge it naturally sweetens it, while the lovely berries kind of just pop when you eat them. Remember, when it comes to beauty and skin support, refined sugar is the enemy and antioxidants and collagen are the superheroes, so this meal has been designed to give you loads of beautifying goodness. Collagen is responsible for plumping and firming the skin, so that's what we're looking for here!

2 cups (200 g) almond meal

¼ teaspoon ground cinnamon

¼ teaspoon ground nutmeg

pinch of salt flakes

1 tablespoon maca powder

2 cups (500 ml) coconut milk

½ cup (60 g) fresh or frozen raspberries

½ cup (75 g) fresh or frozen strawberries, quartered

2–3 drops of stevia (optional)

½ cup (80 g) blueberries

handful of chopped macadamia nuts, to serve

mint leaves, to serve

Heat the almond meal, cinnamon, nutmeg, salt, maca and coconut milk in a small saucepan over a medium heat. Slowly bring to the boil, stirring continuously. Boil for 1 minute, then reduce the heat and simmer for another 2 minutes. Add the raspberries and strawberries and cook for 1 minute more (or 2 minutes if using frozen berries). Taste and, if you'd like it sweeter, stir in a few drops of stevia.

Divide the porridge between two bowls, top with the fresh blueberries and macadamia nuts and scatter with a few torn mint leaves. Tuck on in.

Serves 2

TIP
If you're really craving sweetness (or if you're only just starting to cut sugar out of your diet) adding a few drops of stevia is a great way to sweeten this up without actually adding sugar or having an impact on your blood-glucose levels.

TIP
Feel free to use an
alternative to maple
syrup, such as rice malt
syrup, honey or chopped
dates, if you want things
a little sweeter here.

The bee's knees blueberry pancakes

✳

I love a good pancake creation. Eating pancakes has always been a bit of a tradition for me – when I was living on the Gold Coast and training for a half marathon I used to come home and whip up a batch of these, and the whole family would love them.

3 eggs

2 cups (500 ml) macadamia nut milk

2 cups (260 g) buckwheat flour

1 cup (155 g) frozen blueberries

2 tablespoons maple syrup, plus extra to serve

pinch of ground cinnamon

pinch of salt flakes

2½ tablespoons butter or coconut oil

To serve

fresh blueberries

coconut ice cream

chia seeds (optional)

In a large mixing bowl, whisk together the eggs and macadamia nut milk. Slowly add the buckwheat flour, whisking continuously, until you have a lovely fluffy batter with no lumps. Add the blueberries, maple syrup, cinnamon and salt and mix everything together so that the blueberries are nicely spread throughout the batter.

Melt a teaspoon of the butter or coconut oil in a frying pan over a medium heat. Add a ladleful of batter and wait for 2–3 minutes, or until bubbles appear in the middle of the mixture and the edges crisp up. Flip the pancake with a spatula and cook it for another 2 minutes or so to make sure it's cooked through (you can make sure by using the spatula to lift up a corner of the pancake and taking a sneaky peak underneath). Slide the cooked pancake onto a plate, cover, and repeat with the rest of the batter, adding a teaspoon of butter or coconut oil to the pan between pancakes.

Top the finished pancakes with some fresh blueberries, a scoop of coconut ice cream, a nice glug of maple syrup and a sprinkle of chia seeds, if you like.

Serves 4 (makes 8)

Paleo chocolate, macadamia and zucchini bread

✹

This is perfect for when you are craving chocolate cake but you don't want to undo all of your good work. When I make this little cracker of a recipe, I'll often dive in for seconds – it's really yummy warm, with macadamia butter, cinnamon and maple syrup. The perfect pick-me-up!

½ cup (125 ml) coconut oil, melted, plus extra for greasing

2 zucchini, grated

4 eggs, lightly beaten

⅓ cup (80 ml) maple syrup, plus extra to serve

½ cup (60 g) cacao powder

2 heaped tablespoons coconut flour

½ cup (55 g) almond meal

½ cup (60 g) cacao nibs

½ cup (80 g) macadamia nuts

1 tablespoon maca powder

1 vanilla pod, split and seeds scraped

1 teaspoon ground cinnamon, plus extra to serve

½ teaspoon ground nutmeg

1 teaspoon gluten-free baking powder

pinch of salt flakes

Macadamia butter

3 cups (480 g) macadamia nuts

zest and juice of 1 lemon

½ cup (125 ml) coconut oil, melted

Preheat the oven to 180°C. Grease a 21 cm x 11 cm loaf tin with a little coconut oil.

To make the macadamia butter, pop the macadamias, lemon zest and juice and coconut oil in a food processor and blitz until smooth, blending in a splash of water if it's too thick. Spoon into a bowl or jar (or roll up in baking paper to form a log) and store in the fridge until needed.

Place the grated zucchini in a sieve and press with your hands to remove any excess liquid. Drain on paper towel (or a clean tea towel) and twist to remove the last of the water.

Place the zucchini in a large mixing bowl with the remaining ingredients and mix thoroughly. (The batter should have a nice even consistency and should smell and look quite chocolatey.) Spoon the batter into your loaf tin. Cook for 20–25 minutes, or until a skewer inserted into the centre of the loaf comes out clean.

Remove from the oven and leave to cool before turning out of the tin. Or, if you're like me, wait about 5 minutes, cut a slice, and top it with a slather of the macadamia butter, a drizzle of maple syrup and a sprinkle of cinnamon!

Makes 1 loaf

TIP
This freezes nicely,
too – just slice it up
and pop it in zip-lock
bags in the freezer
until needed.

Super simple rainbow salad with blueberries and macadamias

*

This salad is one of my favourites, not just because it contains so many of the ingredients that I love, but also because it's a walk in the park to make.

There's loads of skin-loving magic in this creation – macadamia nuts with their healthy fats and minerals, plus blueberries for antioxidants, which help to prevent premature skin ageing and free radical damage. It's brilliant on it's own or as a side to your favourite source of protein – if you want to make it a mega skin-boosting meal, think about adding oily fish like salmon or mackerel.

1 bunch of kale, stalks removed and leaves finely chopped

1 avocado, diced

½ cup (60 g) dried blueberries

¼ cup (35 g) chopped macadamia nuts

1 large carrot, grated

zest and juice of 1 lime

2 tablespoons extra-virgin olive oil

salt flakes and freshly ground black pepper

I prepare this in the same bowl I serve it in, so grab a big, beautiful serving bowl. All I do is throw in the kale along with the diced avo, then add the blueberries, macadamias, carrot and lime zest. Give it a good old mix about, dress it with the lime juice and olive oil, season to taste and tuck on in!

Serves 4 as a side

TIP
The dried blueberries give this dish a nice chewy texture, but you can use fresh berries if you prefer.

Mexican chilli beef mole with macadamia quinoa

*

I love Mexican food! I think using spices and chocolate like this is a pretty interesting way to cook, as well as being a brill way to get a truck-load of antioxidants in (these are the guys the skin loves, as they help to prevent early fine lines and wrinkles). Plus you've got your good fats from the macadamia nuts, which really make for a glowing complexion. This recipe also works well with chicken.

⅓ cup (80 ml) extra-virgin olive oil

800 g beef mince

1 red onion, chopped

4 garlic cloves, crushed

6 large tomatoes, chopped

1 red chilli, chopped

1 teaspoon chilli flakes

¼ cup (60 g) almond butter

60 g dark chocolate

1 teaspoon ground cumin

½ teaspoon ground cinnamon

1 teaspoon salt flakes

1 cup (250 ml) beef stock

Macadamia quinoa

2 cups (400 g) quinoa

½ teaspoon coriander seeds

½ bunch of coriander, leaves picked and chopped

zest and juice of 1 lime

⅓ cup (80 ml) extra-virgin olive oil

½ cup (70 g) chopped macadamia nuts

Guacamole

3 avocados

¼ bunch of coriander, leaves picked and chopped

zest and juice of 1 lime

pinch of ground cumin

1 chilli, chopped (optional)

salt flakes and freshly ground black pepper

Heat the olive oil in a large, deep frying pan over a medium heat, add the beef and cook for a few minutes until it begins to brown. Add the onion and garlic and cook until they become translucent.

Now for the magical slow cooker; pop your beef mixture into the slow cooker, add the tomatoes, chilli and chilli flakes, almond butter, chocolate, spices, salt and beef stock. Let this cook gently for up to 6 hours (it will taste amazing after 4 hours, but in my experience the longer it's left, the better it tastes). Now, don't sweat if you don't have a slow cooker; it can also be done on a stovetop. Just add the ingredients to the pan and simmer, with a lid on, over a medium–low heat for 45 minutes, stirring a couple of times to prevent the chocolate from sticking to the bottom of the pan. Remove the lid and simmer for another 45 minutes, stirring occasionally, to reduce the liquid.

While the mole is cooking, make the macadamia quinoa. Rinse the quinoa, then pop it in a pot along with 3 cups (750 ml) of water. Bring the water to the boil, cover with a lid and simmer for 20 minutes (until it has tripled in size and sprouted little tails), then right at the end stir in the coriander seeds. Take it off the heat, stir through the fresh coriander, lime zest and juice, olive oil and macadamia nuts. Cover and set aside.

Finally, make the magic guacamole, which will bring everything together. Scoop the flesh out of the avocados into a bowl and mash with the back of a fork, then add the coriander, lime zest and juice, cumin and chilli, if you like. Season to taste and spoon into a serving bowl. Scoop the chilli mole into a large serving dish and the macadamia quinoa into a pretty bowl. Then it's self-serve, so dig in!

Serves 4–6

Spiced macadamia lamb

✳

This recipe is a goodie for a healthy Sunday night roast. It's a real crowd pleaser and is special enough for that big occasion, but it's also easy enough to just make a big batch and freeze for healthy work lunches!

¼ cup (40 g) macadamia nuts, finely chopped

1 tablespoon sesame seeds

2 teaspoons cumin seeds, crushed

2 teaspoons coriander seeds, crushed

salt flakes and freshly ground black pepper

2 x 500 g lamb back straps, cut in half

2 tablespoons coconut oil or rice bran oil

4 flat mushrooms, washed

1 bunch of kale, stalks removed and leaves finely sliced

2 tablespoons extra-virgin olive oil

juice of ½ lemon

Preheat the oven to 180°C. Combine the macadamia nuts, sesame seeds, cumin and coriander on a plate and season to taste. Coat the lamb back straps with the spiced macadamia mixture.

Heat 1 tablespoon of the coconut or rice bran oil in a large frying pan over a high heat. Add the coated lamb pieces and cook for 2 minutes on each side, or until golden. Transfer to an oven tray and bake until cooked to your liking (about 8 minutes for medium). Remove from the oven and set aside to rest while you cook the vegetables.

Preheat a chargrill or barbecue plate to medium–high. In a large bowl, toss the mushrooms and kale in the remaining coconut or rice bran oil. Transfer to the grill and cook for 2 minutes on each side, or until tender.

Place the vegetables on a platter, drizzle with the olive oil, squeeze over the lemon juice and season well with salt and pepper.

To serve, divide the vegetables among four plates and top with the lamb pieces, cut into thick slices.

Serves 4

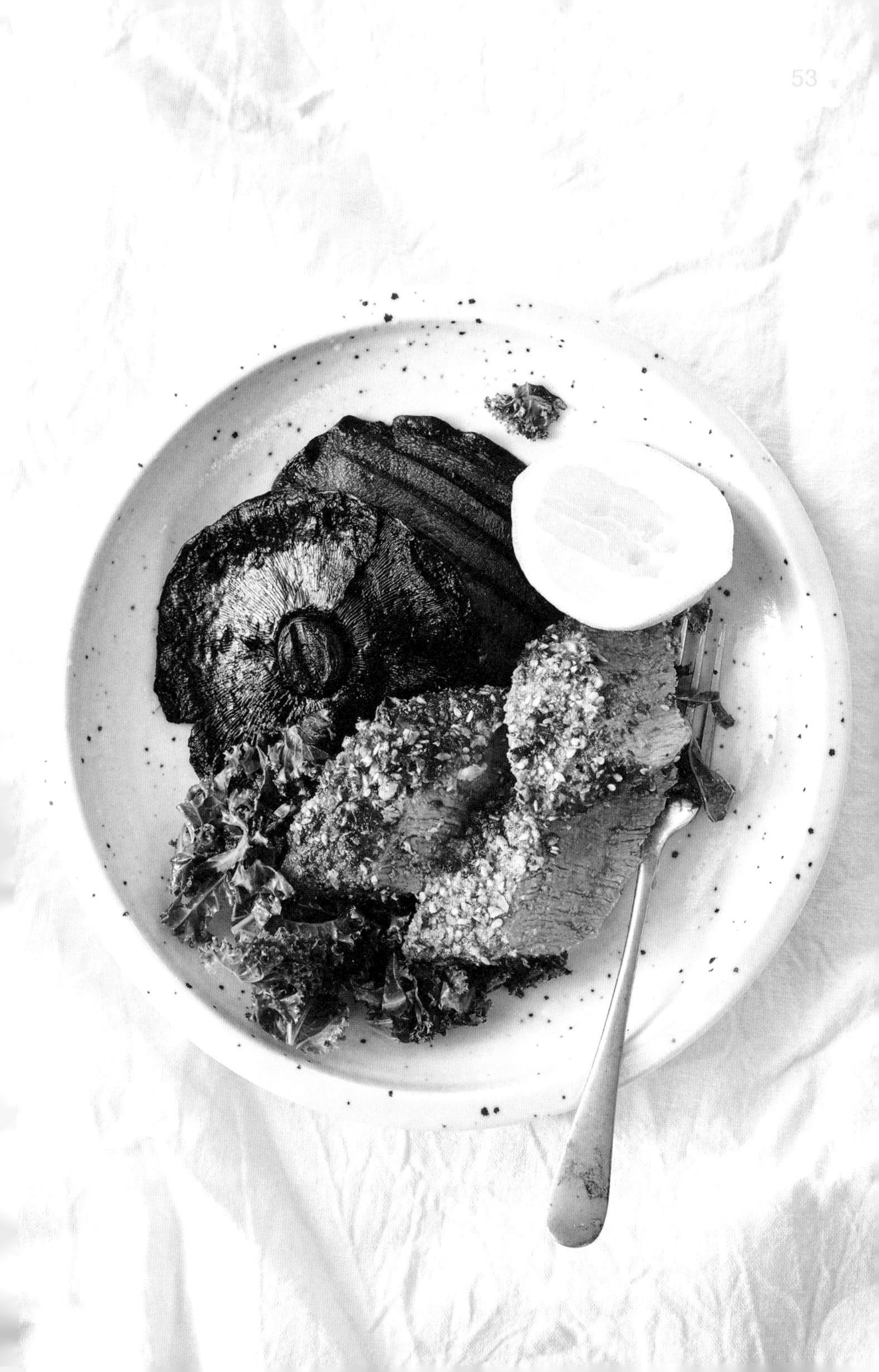

Salted raw chocolate macaroons

These little gems are super easy to make – perfect for when those arvo sugar cravings kick in. They also make sweet little pressies and look great piled up in a jar and tied with a cute ribbon. I love edible pressies …

⅓ cup (40 g) cacao powder

2 tablespoons coconut oil, melted

1 tablespoon hulled tahini

2 tablespoons maple syrup

2 handfuls of coconut flakes

handful of macadamia nuts

pinch of salt flakes

small handful of a mixture of dried cranberries, blueberries and goji berries

Mix the cacao, coconut oil, tahini and maple syrup together until you get a thick paste. Mix the remaining ingredients through, roll into rustic macaroon shapes, place on a lined baking tray and put in the fridge to set (it will only take an hour or so). Keep in an airtight container in the fridge for 1–2 weeks.

Makes 10

TIP
If you want to make these macaroons low in fructose, simply swap out the maple syrup for rice malt syrup.

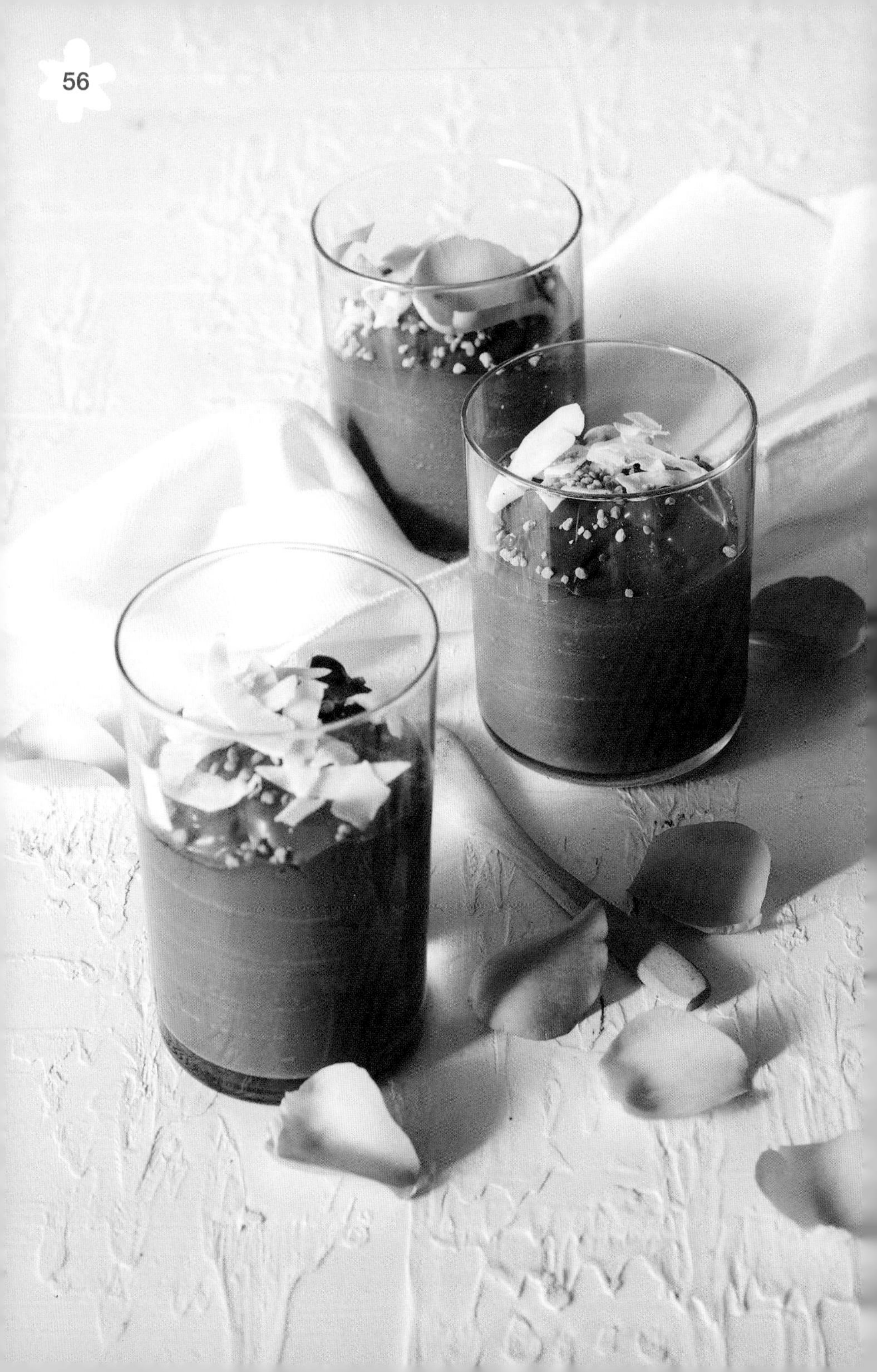

Choc–coconut raw mousse

✶

This recipe was created for the menu at Happy Place, the smoothie bar I own in Melbourne, and it's been so popular that I felt I should share it with you here. It's also very easy to make and is perfect for when those chocolate cravings come calling!

2 ½ avocados

400 ml coconut cream

½ cup (60 g) cacao powder, plus 2 extra tablespoons

½ cup (125 ml) maple syrup

1 tablespoon rice malt syrup

pinch of salt flakes

1 teaspoon vanilla paste

Toppings

bee pollen

coconut flakes

edible flowers

Scoop the flesh out of the avocados into a blender or food processor, add the rest of the ingredients and pulse until smooth and creamy. Spoon into a serving bowl or individual glasses and transfer to the fridge to cool for 2 hours before serving, then make it pretty with your favourite toppings (I like to have mine with bee pollen, coconut flakes and a few edible flowers).

Serves 4–5

Raw white chocolate and mixed berry cheesecake

✽

This is such a pretty dessert and it wows my guests every time. Most people don't even realise it's healthy – I often don't tell them it's raw and vegan until they've devoured it and they don't believe it! It works well as cute little tartlets, too.

Base

½ cup (55 g) almond meal

8 medjool dates, pitted

¼ cup (25 g) desiccated coconut

2 tablespoons almond butter

pinch of salt flakes

White choc filling

2 cups (310 g) cashews, pre-soaked (see page 34)

1 cup (250 ml) almond milk

½ cup (125 ml) maple syrup (or coconut nectar)

¼ cup (185 g) cacao butter, melted

pinch of salt flakes

Berry swirl

¼ cup (40 g) fresh or frozen blueberries

¼ cup (40 g) fresh or frozen raspberries

To decorate

pomegranate seeds

edible rose petals

For the base, place all of the ingredients in a blender with 2 tablespoons of water and blend. You want a tacky, sticky mixture, so if it's not quite there then add another tablespoon or so of water. When the mixture is ready, press it onto the base of a 20 cm springform cake tin, then pop it in the freezer until the filling is ready.

To make the white choc filling, place the cashews, almond milk and maple syrup in a blender and whiz. Pour in the melted cacao butter and salt and blend again. Set aside ½ cup (125 ml) of the filling and pour the remainder onto the cake base, then put the cake tin back in the freezer to begin setting.

To make the berry swirl, place the reserved white choc filling, the blueberries and raspberries in a blender and mix. Pour the berry mixture into a squeeze bottle with a thin nozzle. Take your cake out of the freezer (it doesn't matter if it's not totally set) then pipe the berry mixture in polka dots (or any pattern you like) over the cake.

Place the cake in the fridge for 6 hours or the freezer for 2 hours to set. When set, carefully remove from the tin and place on a serving platter. Decorate with pomegranate seeds and rose petals. Let the cake come to room temperature for 15 minutes before serving.

Serves 12

HOMEMADE
FACE
TREATMENTS

Green glower anti-ageing mask

I love doing this mask last thing at night, but you can do it any time of the day. The honey has antibacterial properties and the spirulina is not only full of anti-ageing antioxidants but is also about 57 per cent protein, so the face will really thrive after having this little treatment. I apply this once or twice a week all over my face, neck and décolletage (and shoulders if they've been exposed to the sun, as they love the extra attention, too).

1 teaspoon fine salt

1 tablespoon spirulina powder

1 tablespoon psyllium husk

2 tablespoons raw honey

Pop the salt, spirulina and psyllium husk into a small bowl and mix to combine, then add the honey. It will feel claggy and hard to combine, but keep mixing, adding 2–4 tablespoons of water, until you get a nice smooth paste.

Apply to a clean face and leave on for 10 minutes. Wash off, pat your face dry and enjoy the glow.

TIP This keeps for about 3 days in the fridge, but the consistency is best if used straight away.

Cinnamon spice exfoliating mask

I love exfoliation masks and try to do them about once per week. I will say this: it can get a tad messy because there are 'bits' in there, but just apply it over the basin or in the shower.

2 tablespoons macadamia oil

2 tablespoons raw sugar

1 tablespoon finely crushed cacao nibs

pinch of ground cinnamon

pinch of ground nutmeg

pinch of ground allspice

Mix all your goodies in a bowl, then apply to a clean face in circular motions with the pads of your fingertips for a couple of minutes (about the length of your favourite song). Wash off and pat your face dry. You'll feel really fresh after this little number. It can leave the skin feeling a little oily, so you may need a double wash.

Deep-cleansing clay mask

This mask deeply cleanses and smooths the face and neck. The naturally occurring lactic acid in the yoghurt helps to tighten and tone the skin, while the honey has powerful antioxidant and antibacterial properties.

¼ cup (60 g) bentonite clay

¼ cup (60 g) plain yoghurt

2 tablespoons raw honey

pinch of dulse flakes

1 tablespoon coconut oil, melted

Place all the ingredients in a bowl, mix thoroughly, then apply evenly around the face and neck, avoiding the eyes – I pop a hand towel around my shoulders, so it doesn't get too messy! I also put this on the backs of my hands to help prevent ageing.) Leave it on for 5 minutes before rinsing off. This will make enough for five masks.

TIP If you're not using it straight away, this will keep in an airtight container in the fridge for 3–4 days.

THREE

EYES

RECIPES AND REMEDIES

Hero ingredients

I like to put a lot of effort into looking after my eyes, as it tends to be where people age first. I love smile lines – I think they show happiness and love – but if I can prevent deep crow's feet by using eye oils and serums, then I'm all for it! They say our eyes are the windows to our soul – pretty special, hey? – so let's look after them and keep them extra sparkly.

Avocados

Avos and anti-ageing go hand in hand for both topical use and in our diets. I would go as far as saying that avocados are one of my all-time favourite foods – I could live off them. In fact, some say you actually can, as they're one of the most nutrient-dense foods on the planet! From a beauty perspective, good fats are one of the keys to ageing gracefully, and the humble avocado is full of them.

Cucumbers

We've all seen movies where the leading lady is at a day spa with a facemask on and cucumber slices over her eyes, right? Well, it is true that the good old cucumber is brilliant for preventing puffiness around the eyes. They have a cooling and smoothing effect (I even use them topically on sunburn and they're awesome). On top of this, they're also a great source of silica, which has been taken internally as a beauty supplement for as long as I can remember. We need silica for connective tissue health and therefore collagen formation thrives when we have silica in our bodies.

Prunes

These guys are an incredibly cheap
superfood. They're extremely high in
antioxidants, which we know are the key
to skin health and preventing free radical
damage. Antioxidants in supplement form
or even in other superfoods such as goji
berries or acai are awesome, but can get
a bit costly, and so I bring you the humble
prune, which contains double the amount
of antioxidants found in blueberries on
the Oxygen Radical Absorbance Capacity
(ORAC) scale (see page 166). By upping
the prunes in your life you're also upping the
youth-promoting antioxidants. Try adding
them to your brekkie for more than just
your daily fibre fix!

Cucumber, mango and mint slushie

I love to whip up this slushie when I'm after something really refreshing in a hurry. If you feel like a more adult creation, try adding a dash of vodka to this!

1 Lebanese cucumber, roughly chopped

1 mango, flesh roughly chopped

½ bunch of mint, leaves picked

zest and juice of 1 lime

1 cup ice cubes

Pop everything into your blender and blitz it up to a slushie-like consistency. Pour into glasses and enjoy!

Serves 2

Glowy bircher

✱

This is a brilliant all-round anti-ageing dish, not just because of the antioxidants and fibre the prunes contain, but also because I've added a hint of turmeric, which also has antioxidant, anti-inflammatory and anti-ageing properties (as well as giving it a nice yellowy-orange colour).

1 cup (100 g) rolled oats

¼ cup (40 g) almonds, roughly chopped

¼ cup (30 g) walnuts, roughly chopped

¼ cup (40 g) chia seeds, plus extra to serve

¼ cup (30 g) sultanas

¼ cup (45 g) pitted and chopped dates

¼ cup (60 g) pitted and chopped dried prunes, plus extra to serve

½ teaspoon ground cinnamon

¼ teaspoon ground nutmeg

½ teaspoon ground turmeric

1½ cups (375 ml) almond milk or coconut milk

1 granny smith apple, grated

½ cup (140 g) of your favourite coconut yoghurt, plus extra to serve

maple syrup, to serve

Pop all of the dry ingredients in a large bowl and combine (it's going to look like a regular muesli mix at this stage). Mix through the spices and almond or coconut milk, then cover and place in the fridge to soak overnight.

In the morning, fold through the grated apple, then fold through the yoghurt. Divide among bowls, top with an extra dollop of yoghurt, a couple of prunes and a sprinkle of chia seeds, and finish it off with a drizzle of maple syrup.

Serves 4–6

TIPS
If you want to keep things
gluten free, switch out the
rolled oats for quinoa flakes.
And if you don't have any
dairy allergies, then
full-cream yoghurt works
wonders here, too.

Anti-ageing avo salad with pink dressing

✳

I love this salad, not only because it looks super bright and ticks all the eye-health boxes, but because it tastes amazing. It works as both a side dish and as a great stand-alone veggo meal.

2 bunches of baby spinach, washed and dried

1 avocado, sliced

½ cup (65 g) dried cranberries

2 celery stalks, chopped

½ cup (60 g) roughly chopped walnuts

½ punnet (125 g) strawberries, sliced

1 punnet (125 g) raspberries

Pink dressing

¼ cup (60 ml) apple cider vinegar

½ cup (125 ml) extra-virgin olive oil

1 teaspoon dijon mustard

½ punnet (125 g) strawberries

salt flakes and freshly ground black pepper

I have a little trick with the assembly of this salad. Get a round serving platter and cover the base of it with the baby spinach. Then, in different sections (like you were building a pie chart), place all the rest of the salad ingredients around the platter neatly in their own little sections.

In a blender or food processor, whiz together your dressing ingredients until smooth, then drizzle the pink dressing over the salad just before serving. Pretty!

Serves 4

Vegan sushi rolls

✳

These rolls make a fun little snack. They look great, taste great and we're using cauliflower instead of rice so they're also paleo. On top of that, these rolls are totally vegan, but of course you can tweak them to suit your own tastebuds, too.

1 head of cauliflower, roughly chopped

1 garlic clove (optional)

salt flakes and freshly ground black pepper

1 packet nori sheets

gluten-free tamari or soy sauce, for dipping (optional)

Filling

1 avocado, cut into thick wedges

1 Lebanese cucumber, cut into batons

1 carrot, grated

2 beetroot, grated

¼ cup (40 g) sesame seeds, toasted

Pop your cauliflower chunks into a food processor and blitz until the mixture resembles grains of rice. Place a saucepan of water over a medium heat, add the cauliflower and garlic, if using, and simmer for 10 minutes, or until the cauliflower has just softened. Drain thoroughly, discard the garlic clove, season with salt and pepper and leave to cool slightly (just so it's not too hot to handle), then place the cauliflower mixture between two sheets of paper towel and press firmly to absorb as much excess water as possible.

Now it's time to assemble. Lay a nori sheet down on a clean work surface and cover it with a layer of cauli rice, leaving a few centimetres free on the side furthest away from you. In the centre of the sheet, arrange a selection of your lovely filling ingredients neatly in a line, sprinkling over the sesame seeds, then roll it up nice and tight. Repeat with the rest of the cauli rice, nori sheets and filling ingredients, then slice your sushi roll into discs. Dip them into tamari or soy sauce, if you like, and enjoy straight away!

Serves 4

TIP
You can use up any leftover nori sheets by crushing them up and sprinkling them over salads.

Best pumpkin dip in town!

This recipe was inspired by my mate Kemi, who is pretty amazing in the kitchen and knows how to make some seriously yummy raw food creations. I don't just use this as a dip, I also love adding it to sandwiches and wraps – it's full of flavour and nutritionally it ticks all the boxes. It also makes a great side to any protein.

1 cup (155 g) roughly chopped butternut pumpkin

1 cup (155 g) roughly chopped zucchini

½ cup (80 g) roughly chopped red or yellow capsicum

2 tablespoons pumpkin seeds

2 tablespoons olive oil

2 tomatoes, finely diced

1 tablespoon sweet paprika

1 tablespoon finely chopped green chilli

1 tablespoon lemon juice

1 garlic clove, crushed

1 teaspoon ground coriander

1 teaspoon finely chopped ginger

¼ teaspoon salt flakes, plus extra

3 tablespoons finely chopped flat-leaf parsley leaves

1 large avocado

Dippers

2 carrots, cut into batons

1 yellow capsicum, cut into long wedges

4 baby cucumbers, cut into batons

Pop the pumpkin, zucchini, capsicum, pumpkin seeds and olive oil in a food processor and pulse until the mixture has the texture of chunky pesto. Spoon into a bowl, add all the remaining ingredients except the avocado and mix everything together well. Place in the fridge and allow the flavours to infuse for 1 hour.

Scoop the avocado into a bowl, mash roughly with the back of a fork and sprinkle with salt. Divide the pumpkin mix among four bowls and top each with a spoonful of avocado. Use your veggie dippers to tuck in.

Serves 4

Japanese cucumber salad

✸

This salad is fresh, minimal and cleansing. In Japan, it's eaten as an appetiser, but I like it as a side with other salads and protein. It's traditionally made with rice vinegar and sugar, but this is my super healthy spin on it!

4 cucumbers

large handful of cucamelons (optional)

¼ cup (60 ml) apple cider vinegar

1 teaspoon rice malt syrup

¼ teaspoon salt flakes

⅓ cup (50 g) sesame seeds, toasted

Use a vegetable peeler or mandoline to peel the outer fleshy part of the cucumber into really fine, long strips. Most people remove the skin but I keep it on (most of the nutritional value can be found there), just discarding the central seeds. Pop the cucumber strips into a bowl with the cucamelons (if using).

In a small bowl, mix together the apple cider, rice malt syrup and salt until the salt has dissolved.

Pour the dressing over the cucumber and massage it lightly with your fingertips, then pile it onto a serving plate and scatter over the sesame seeds to finish.

Serves 4 as a side

Baked avo chippies with real mayo

✳

Avocado chips are turning into one of my favourite snacks. I work with Grill'd (the healthy burger joint) and when they asked me to taste-test their avo chips I was hooked. These ones are quite different to those at Grill'd, but it was there that I fell in love with them for the first time. Some people are funny about warm avo (I used to be), but trust me, once you try these you won't look back!

2 eggs (or 1 egg plus egg whites from Real Mayo below), lightly beaten

2 cups (160 g) gluten-free dried breadcrumbs

2 avocados, halved, each half sliced into 4 wedges and peeled

lime wedges, to serve

Real mayo

2 egg yolks

juice of 1 lemon

pinch of salt flakes

200 ml mild extra-virgin olive oil

1 tablespoon dijon mustard

Preheat the oven to 180°C and line a baking tray with baking paper.

Place the beaten egg in one small bowl and the breadcrumbs in another. Dip the avocado wedges first in the egg and then in the crumbs to coat evenly, then lay the pieces out on your baking tray, leaving space between them so they cook nice and evenly. Bake for 7 minutes on one side, then flip and cook for another 5 minutes, or until they are nice and golden at the edges.

While the chippies are cooking, whip up your mayo. Start by whizzing the egg yolks and lemon juice together in a food processor. Once the mix starts to thicken, add the salt, oil and mustard and continue to blitz until the mixture is nice and creamy. Spoon the mayo out into a serving dish or little bowl.

Once the avo chippies are cooked, arrange them on a big plate or in a bowl, squeezing over some fresh lime juice and serving them alongside the mayo for dipping.

Serves 2–4

Moroccan lamb and prune tagine

✳

It's so nice to use prunes in this kind of dish – it just takes everything to a whole new level! Now, this recipe isn't just a brilliant source of antioxidants, it's also full of fibre and protein, so it should help to keep you sustained and full for a long period of time, making it the perfect lunch or dinner meal. The cinnamon will also help to balance your blood-sugar levels, so you should find you won't be needing an after-dinner treat when you have this.

⅓ cup (80 ml) coconut oil

2 onions, chopped

1 teaspoon ground nutmeg

1 teaspoon ground cinnamon

1 teaspoon ground turmeric

1 × 1.2 kg boneless leg of lamb, cut into cubes

1 cup (220 g) prunes, pitted and roughly chopped

200 ml pomegranate juice

salt flakes and freshly ground black pepper

1 head of cauliflower, separated into florets

½ bunch of flat-leaf parsley, leaves picked and roughly chopped

¼ cup (30 g) chopped walnuts

Heat 3 tablespoons of the coconut oil in a large, heavy-based saucepan or tagine over a low heat. Add the onion and cook for 8–10 minutes until softened, then stir in the spices and turn up the heat to high.

Add the lamb to the pan and brown on all sides, then add the prunes, pomegranate juice and 300 ml of water and season to taste. Bring to the boil, then reduce to a simmer and cook, covered with a lid, for 1 hour 45 minutes. Remove the lid for and cook for another 15 minutes, until the lamb is tender and falling apart and the sauce has reduced nicely. Check the tagine regularly during cooking, adding extra water if the lamb looks like it is drying out.

15 minutes before the lamb is ready, pop the cauliflower chunks into a food processor and blitz until the mixture resembles grains of rice.

Heat the remaining coconut oil in a frying pan over a medium heat, add the cauliflower rice and sauté for 3–5 minutes until it is just tender but still has a slight crunch (be careful not to overcook it). Season to taste.

To serve, divide the cauli rice among bowls and spoon over the lamb tagine. Sprinkle with freshly chopped parsley and walnuts and dig in immediately.

Serves 4

TIPS
In Australia, we have access
to pretty moist prunes, but
if yours are super dry, try
soaking them in water for
15 minutes. You can use any
sweetener you like instead of
coconut sugar here – rice malt
syrup, maple syrup, honey or
dates all work well.

Prune and chocolate fudge brownie slice

✿

Really easy and super fudgy, these guys are my perfect 3 pm pick-me-up treat!
You might think they will taste too pruney, but not at all – in fact, it's the prunes that
make them so fudgy. These brownies are a great way to sneak extra antioxidants and
fibre into your diet, plus they're gluten free, dairy free, grain free, paleo and vegan –
so they should keep everyone happy no matter what kind of eating plan they're on.
I also include brazil nuts for the bonus skin support the good fats and
antioxidants they contain bring.

1 cup (220 g) prunes, pitted

1 cup (250 ml) coconut milk

¼ cup (60 ml) coconut oil, melted

1 cup (100 g) almond meal

¼ cup (30 g) cacao powder

½ cup (100 g) coconut sugar

pinch of salt flakes

½ cup (70 g) roughly chopped brazil nuts

coconut ice cream, to serve (optional)

Preheat the oven to 180°C and line a 28 cm x 21 cm
baking tray with baking paper.

Pop the prunes into a food processor and pulse until finely
chopped, then add everything else, except the brazil nuts
and ice cream, and whiz together to form a thick, super-
sticky batter. Add most of the brazil nuts and pulse for
a few seconds just to spread them through the mixture
(you don't want to chop them up further because they
give the brownies a great texture). Scoop out the mixture
with a spatula onto your baking tray and level it out nicely.
Top with the remaining brazil nuts.

Bake the brownies in the oven for 20–25 minutes, or until
cooked on the outside but still a little bit sticky and fudgy
in the middle (if you like them cooked all the way through,
leave them in there for 30 minutes). Remove from the
oven and leave to cool, then cut into pieces and serve
with some coconut ice cream – or just enjoy them on
their own!

Makes 16

Oozy sticky date and prune pud

✱

I've created this recipe in honour of my dad, whose favourite treat is sticky date pudding; no matter where I am, whenever I see it on a menu I always think of him. The reason why I'm so excited about this dessert is that I've made it healthier by including prunes, which ups the fibre and antioxidants. It's a great way to 'trick' people into eating prunes because it's so yummy and, I'll admit, I was a little blown away by it because – just like my awesome dad – I think a great sticky date pud is hard to top!

1 cup (250 ml) coconut oil, plus extra for greasing

1 cup (220 g) prunes, pitted and chopped

1 cup (180 g) medjool dates, pitted and chopped

1½ cups (155 g) almond meal

½ teaspoon ground cinnamon

¼ teaspoon ground nutmeg

½ teaspoon gluten-free baking powder

pinch of salt flakes

5 eggs, lightly beaten

2 tablespoons apple cider vinegar

coconut ice cream, to serve (optional but highly recommended!)

Preheat the oven to 160°C. Grease a 32 cm x 24 cm baking tin with coconut oil.

Place the prunes and dates in a saucepan with 2 cups (500 ml) of water and bring to the boil. Reduce the heat and simmer for 5 minutes, then remove from the heat and stir in the coconut oil. Leave to cool slightly, then transfer to a food processor and blend to form a smooth paste. Set aside.

Combine the almond meal, cinnamon, nutmeg, baking powder and salt in a large bowl. Fold through the egg and apple cider vinegar, then stir in half of the date paste to form a batter.

Pour all but ½ cup (125 ml) of the remaining date mixture onto the base of the tin (the ½ cup is to use as a sauce at the end). Now pour over the almond meal batter. Bake for 30 minutes.

Remove the pud from the oven. Serve into bowls while it's still a little warm. Spoon over any sauce left in the baking tin and serve with coconut ice cream, if you like, with the remaining datey sauce warmed up and served alongside.

Serves 10

TIP
Leftovers
freeze well – if
you have any!

HOMEMADE EYE TREATMENTS

Bright eyes syrup

This little syrup helps to soothe and plump the delicate under-eye area for a youthful look. To be honest, I use this one most nights — it's a go-to for me! This will keep for ages in a sealed jar.

¼ cup (60 ml) extra-virgin olive oil

2 tablespoons rosehip oil

4 drops of rose essential oil

Mix the oils together and store in a sealed glass jar until needed.

To use, gently apply a little of the syrup around the eye sockets. Leave on for 5 minutes, then pat off with a clean towel. If you want to wear the eye syrup to bed (that's what I do) just do this after your night-time skin routine. This will make about a month's worth. Store it in the bathroom cabinet.

Rosehip oil drops

I like to add a few drops of rose essential oil to this recipe (you'll see it's optional below) as it makes this treatment smell so enticing. In fact, it's said that one of the reasons Cleopatra was so adored by men was that she would put on a few drops of rose oil and they were able to smell her scent before she arrived. So bring on the rose oil, I say!

¼ cup (60 ml) rosehip oil

¼ cup (60 ml) jojoba oil

3 drops of rose essential oil (optional)

Mix everything together and store in a dark glass jar away from sunlight (it will keep for ages, and storing it out of the light will make it last longer).

To apply, use your ring finger to gently pat the mixture around your eyes. Leave on for 10 minutes, then wash off or wear it to bed (that's what I do). I also rub it into my neck and décolletage. This will make enough for about 2 months – keep it in the fridge.

Youth elixir

This one can be used just around your eyes, but I like to use it all over my face. It is quite oily, so just be mindful that it can leave a mark on your pillow if you wear it to bed (which I do). This concoction will be solid in winter, but it will soften in the warmer months.

¼ cup (60 g) shea butter

1 teaspoon apple cider vinegar

¼ cup (60 ml) argan oil

¼ cup (60 ml) cacao butter, broken into chunks

½ cup (60 ml) coconut oil

You will need to stir this concoction constantly as you make it. Start by setting a heatproof bowl over a saucepan filled with 2 cm of just-simmering water. Add the cacao butter and stir to melt (it'll take 4–5 minutes, depending on the size of the chunks). Once melted, add the coconut oil and then the shea butter. Once both have melted, take the bowl off the heat. Now add the argan oil, stir for about 10 seconds and then add the apple cider vinegar. After a final stir, pour the mixture into a wide-mouth glass jar. It will harden at room temperature after a few days, so use a spoon to scoop it out and the mixture will melt with the warmth of your hands. Note: this may not be the yummiest smelling thing, but it really works wonders and I use it daily!

FOUR

SKIN

RECIPES AND REMEDIES

Hero ingredients

Your skin is your largest organ and it really does absorb what you put on it. I love the theory that you should only put stuff on your face/body that you'd also be willing to put *in* your face. And by that I mean food! I know this sounds really hippie, but if your skin absorbs around 65 per cent of what you put on it topically (see page 166), then it's worth being pretty conscious about what goes on it.

Coffee

You may be surprised to see coffee in here. I have only recently become a coffee drinker, and there are healthy and not-so-healthy ways to drink it. If you're adding loads of sugar and cow's milk then the health benefits aren't quite so high; however, if you're drinking it black or with a dash of almond milk, then we're talking. Coffee is one of the highest antioxidant-containing foods available and those antioxidants aren't affected by heat, which is brilliant! You can have too much of a good thing when it comes to coffee, however, and if you do have too much it can over-stimulate your stress hormone cortisol, so aim for no more than 1–2 cups a day.

Extra-virgin olive oil

This is a staple in almost every kitchen, but it has also been used topically for yonks. It's known as a skin healer and is said to help promote soft and smooth skin. There are remedies for putting a capful in the bathtub to help with eczema, and post showering as a moisturiser. Extra-virgin olive oil even contains this stuff called squalene, which is a powerful antioxidant that helps to prevent UV damage and has been known to have anti-ageing effects. Squalene is otherwise quite hard to find naturally in food sources.

Walnuts

Walnuts contain a nice hit of both mono-
unsaturated fats and omega 3 fatty acids,
which the skin thrives off, as they help
to strengthen the cell membranes and
therefore to retain moisture. On top of
that, they contain vitamin E, which helps to
keep the skin smooth and glowing. They're
a great source of vegetarian protein, too,
which we need for tissue repair, so walnuts
are an all-round skin-boosting food in my
eyes. One of my favourite snacks is to
remove the pit from a medjool date, stuff
it with a walnut and then sprinkle it with
cinnamon – it's delish and kicks the sugar
cravings at the same time!

Coffee chai

✳

I am really excited about this recipe because I'm new to loving coffee – I guess you'd say I'm a late bloomer. You see, my partners at Happy Place (my smoothie bar), Salvatore Malatesta and Lachlan Ward, are both Melbourne coffee gurus and I've learned so much from them about the art of coffee. It's now a ritual that I treasure mindfully every day (and being full of antioxidant health benefits, it's great for brain function, too). The truth is, if it wasn't for them I wouldn't have ever tried coffee, so here's a recipe for coffee chai inspired by my coffee heroes.

20 g coarsely ground coffee (a mortar and pestle will do the job)

1–3 cups (250–750 ml) boiling water

almond milk, to serve (optional)

Chai mix

1 tablespoon cardamom pods

1 cinnamon stick, broken into small pieces

1 teaspoon fennel seeds

4 star anise

1 tablespoon cacao nibs

2 tablespoons honey

1 teaspoon vanilla paste

1 teaspoon grated ginger

To make the chai mix, pop the spices in a frying pan over a medium heat and toast for 3–4 minutes, or until aromatic and sweet. Remove from the heat, tip into a mortar and crush with a pestle into smaller pieces. Add the rest of the ingredients, along with 1 teaspoon of water and the coffee, and stir together, ensuring that all the ingredients are coated in honey and the mix is looking moist (add a little extra water if necessary).

To serve, combine 1 cup (250 ml) of hot water with 2 tablespoons of chai mix per person and leave to brew for 3 minutes, then strain into your favourite cups. Enjoy black, or add a splash of almond milk to give it a nutty dimension.

Serves 1–3

Coffee and date smoothie

❋

This is the perfect way to kickstart your day – a delicious creamy coffee smoothie that will keep you full until lunchtime! If you don't like coffee, I can promise you the smoothie still tastes brill without it, so make it work for you. The dates and banana are also great sources of fibre and act like an intestinal broom.

4 medjool dates, pitted

1 frozen banana (peel it before you freeze it)

2 tablespoons almond butter

1 tablespoon coconut oil

1 teaspoon cacao powder

1 shot (30 ml) espresso coffee

2 cups (500 ml) almond milk

Optional toppings

crushed walnuts

ground coffee

Pop everything into your blender and whiz it all together. Pour into glasses, top with a handful of crushed walnuts and a sprinkling of ground coffee, if desired, and off you go!

Serves 2

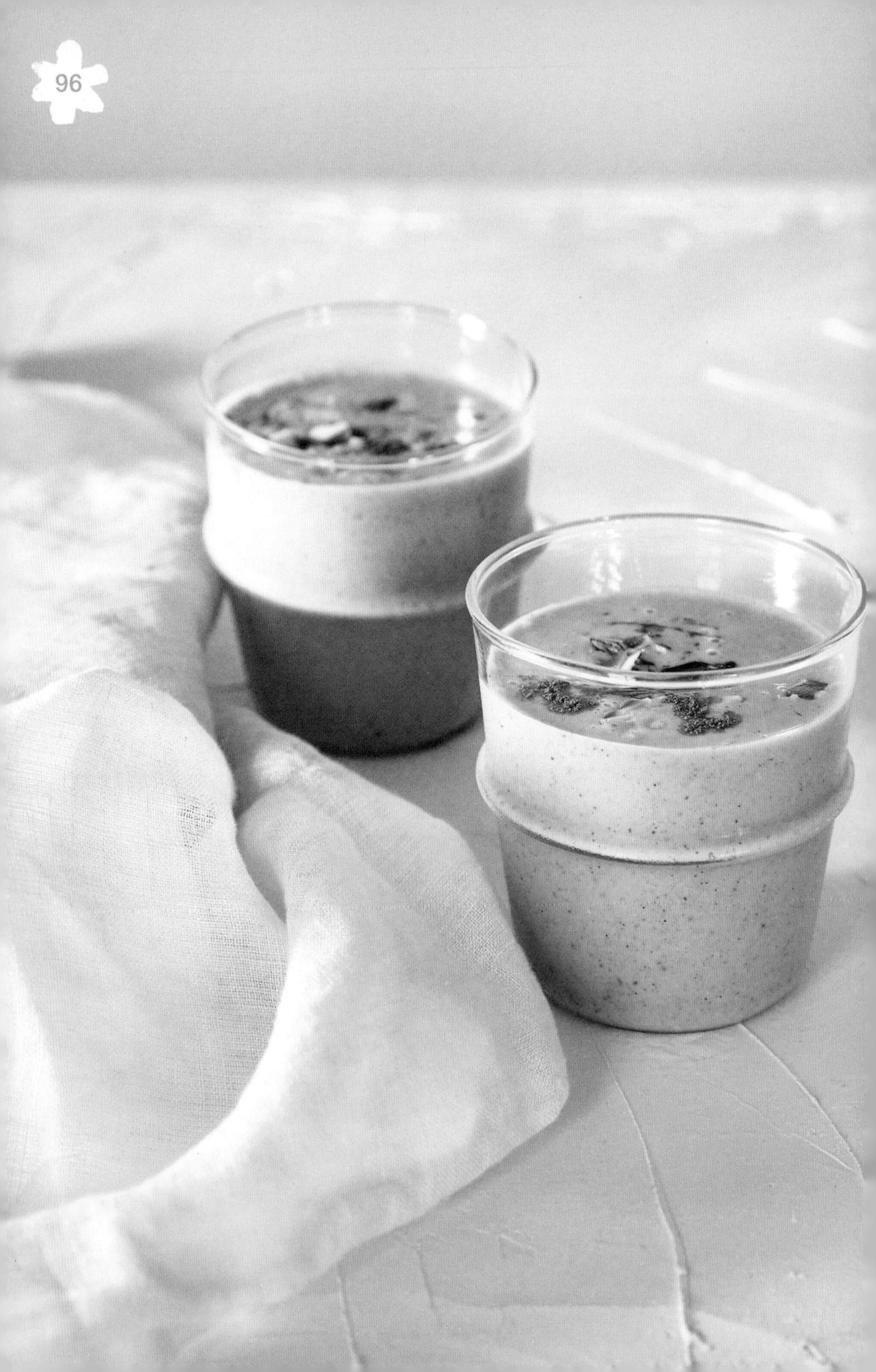

Gingerbread smoothie

✳

This creation also comes from Happy Place, my smoothie bar. We wanted to create
a festive smoothie that tasted like Christmas, and our manager, Bannie, came up with
this little gem. The first time I tried it I was blown away – it tastes like you're drinking
a gingerbread man – and it was so popular we had to keep it on the menu.
I hope you like it as much as I do!

2 frozen bananas (peel them
before you freeze them)

1 tablespoon almond butter

1 tablespoon maple syrup

1½ teaspoons ginger powder

½ teaspoon ground cinnamon

¼ teaspoon ground nutmeg

½ teaspoon vanilla paste
(or seeds of ½ vanilla pod)

¼ cup (25 g) rolled oats

300 ml almond milk

Toppings

crushed almonds

ground cinnamon

maple syrup

Pop everything into your blender and blend until smooth,
but also nice and thick. Pour into glasses or bowls and top
with a few crushed almonds, a sprinkle of cinnamon and
drizzle of maple syrup. Enjoy!

Serves 2

Skin-booster salad

*

I'm all about making salads interesting, especially when I'm keen to eat super clean or I'm on a cleanse. Try adding some protein to make this more of a main meal for two. I love it alongside two or three poached eggs, my favourite crispy salmon (see page 129), some grilled chicken or even a few yummy lamb cutlets.

2 handfuls of baby spinach

1 pomegranate, seeds popped

½ punnet (125 g) strawberries, sliced

1 cucumber (or 4 baby cucumbers), sliced or peeled into thin ribbons

¼ cup (25 g) mung beans, washed

¼ cup (30 g) sunflower seeds

½ cup (30 g) shredded coconut

pinch of salt flakes and freshly ground black pepper

Dressing

3 tablespoons extra-virgin olive oil

2 tablespoons apple cider vinegar

1 teaspoon wholegrain mustard

Pop all the salad ingredients into a big serving bowl and mix together really well.

Mix the dressing ingredients together in a small bowl to combine. Pour the dressing over the salad and season with salt and pepper, then give everything another good old mix. Serve and enjoy.

Serves 4 as a side

TIP
You can buy packets of pomegranate seeds in some supermarkets, which takes away the mess.

Raw zoodle pasta with walnut pesto and chicken

✳

To be honest, I eat zoodles (or zucchini noodles) most nights – I just love them. The walnuts in the pesto are not only great for our skin, but being high in mono-unsaturated fats, they are also great for brain health. If you think about it, they even look like little brains, which might be a good way to get kids to try them!

3 zucchini, peeled

2 tablespoons extra-virgin olive oil, plus extra to serve

4 chicken thighs, thinly sliced

Walnut pesto

½ cup (80 g) pine nuts, toasted

1 cup (100 g) walnuts

1 cup basil leaves, plus extra to serve

2 garlic cloves

zest and juice of 1 lemon

⅓ cup (80 ml) extra-virgin olive oil

salt flakes and freshly ground black pepper

First, whip up the pesto by putting all the ingredients in a food processor and blitzing until you have the texture you like. Season to taste.

For the pasta, slice the zucchini into noodles using either a mandoline, a veggie spiraliser or a green papaya grater. Pop the zoodles in a big serving bowl and set aside.

Heat the olive oil in a frying pan over a medium heat, add the chicken pieces and fry for 2–3 minutes on each side until cooked – it won't take too long. Add the pesto to the pan, stir everything together and cook for another 3 minutes, then tip your steaming hot pesto chicken over the zucchini noodles and toss so that the chicken heats the noodles. Serve topped with a few basil leaves and a sweet little drizzle of olive oil.

Serves 2

TIP
You could use 2 chicken breasts here instead of the thighs, though if you haven't tried thighs for a while I'd suggest giving them a go as they are really tasty. If you're veggo or vegan then this recipe works a treat without the chicken too!

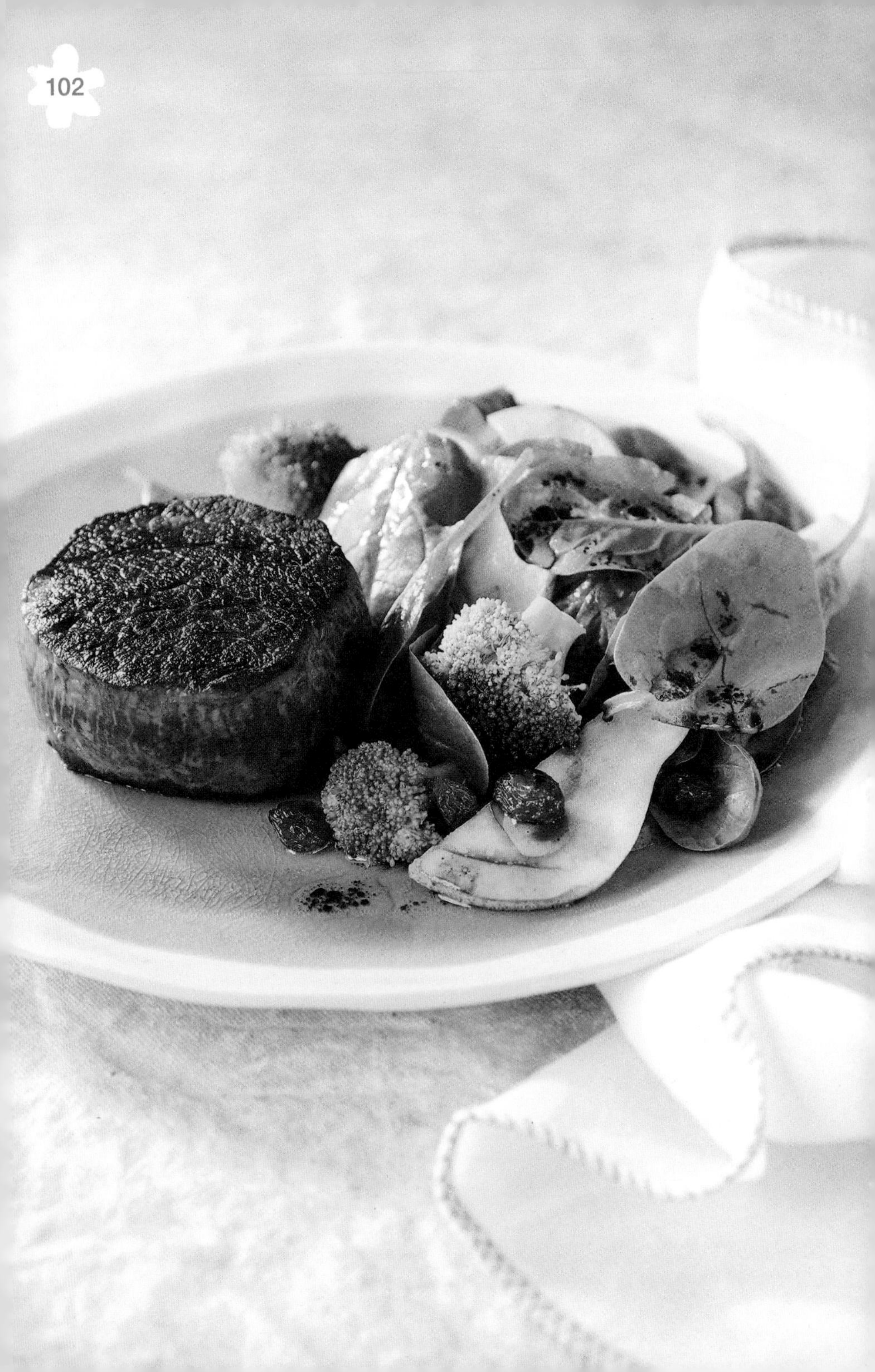

Best steaks ever
with broccoli and pear salad

✳

This is my take on the classic simple Aussie dinner, with the salad jazzing it up a tad.
I love making these steaks to help keep my iron levels up, and I always notice
a complete protein like this helps to prevent any sugar cravings I might have, too.
I sometimes make this salad as a stand-alone and it always hits the spot.

2 tablespoons extra-virgin olive oil or coconut oil

2 x 180–200 g fillet steaks

salt flakes and freshly ground black pepper

Broccoli and pear salad

2 cups (180 g) broccoli florets

handful of baby spinach

1 pear, sliced

3 tablespoons sultanas

½ cup (60 g) walnuts, roughly chopped

3 tablespoons extra-virgin olive oil

1 tablespoon balsamic vinegar

salt flakes and freshly ground black pepper

To make the broccoli and pear salad, bring 2 cups (500 ml) of water to the boil in a saucepan over a medium–high heat. Place the broccoli florets in a steamer, set them over the pan and steam for 3–4 minutes, or until the broccoli has softened but still has a bit of crunch. (It should look bright green.) Set aside to cool.

Once cool, combine the broccoli, baby spinach, pear, sultanas and walnuts in a large bowl. Whisk the olive oil and balsamic vinegar together and season to taste, then pour over the salad and toss together well. Set aside.

Heat the olive oil or coconut oil in a frying pan over a medium heat. Add the steaks to the pan and cook for 3–4 minutes on one side, then turn over and cook for a further 2 minutes. Remove from the heat and leave to rest for 4–5 minutes.

Divide the broccoli and pear salad between two plates and place the steaks alongside. (I always pour the pan juices over the meat for added flavour.) Season to taste with salt and pepper, then dig in.

Serves 2

Paleo red velvet cupcakes

✳

Nourishing your body doesn't mean missing out on your favourite foods, in fact it's quite the opposite – it's about replacing the treats with healthier options and never depriving yourself. I love these little gems because they're both delicious and seriously pretty (I love the little flecks of beet you get through the cake). It's so lovely to enjoy a sweet treat knowing that your body will be humming afterwards because it's been made from real wholefoods. My advice would be to soak up every single second you're enjoying this delicious healthy creation.

250 g (2–3) raw beetroot, grated (keep the skin on)

3 eggs

2 cups (200 g) almond meal

1 vanilla pod, split and seeds scraped (or ¼ teaspoon vanilla powder or extract)

pinch of salt flakes

¼ cup (30 g) cacao powder

⅓ cup (80 ml) extra-virgin olive oil

½ cup (125 ml) maple syrup or honey

½ cup (80 g) sultanas

½ teaspoon baking soda

handful of walnuts, roughly chopped, plus extra to decorate (optional)

Icing

1 cup (250 g) softened cream cheese

½ cup (125 ml) maple syrup

Preheat the oven to 180°C and line a 12-hole muffin tray with paper cases.

Place all the ingredients in a large bowl and mix together really well to form a batter. Scoop the mixture evenly into the paper cases (I use an ice-cream scoop) and bake for 40–45 minutes, or until a skewer inserted in the middle of a cupcake comes out clean. Remove from the oven and leave to cool.

While the cupcakes are cooling, make the icing. In a small bowl, combine the cream cheese and maple syrup and beat until smooth. Ice the cooled cupcakes and top with some extra walnut halves, if desired. Yum!

Makes 12

Lucky cookie sandwiches

✳

I call these lucky cookie sandwiches because they're full of so much nutrition, how could they not bring good luck?! They're naturally really high in fibre, as well as containing antioxidants and good fats, plus they taste like magic. I've found that these ones are a real winner with the kidlets. Tip: the cookies on their own are delish, as is the filling.

2 ½ cups (250 g) rolled oats

1 banana, mashed

½ cup (60 g) roughly chopped walnuts

½ cup (60 g) sultanas

1 cup (150 g) grated apple

2 tablespoons maple syrup

1 vanilla pod, split and seeds scraped (or ¼ teaspoon vanilla powder or extract)

2 tablespoons coconut oil, melted

2 tablespoons almond butter

½ teaspoon ground cinnamon

¼ teaspoon ground nutmeg

pinch of salt flakes

Filling

1 cup (155 g) cashews, pre-soaked (see page 34)

½ cup (45 g) desiccated coconut

pinch of salt flakes

2 tablespoons coconut oil, melted

2 tablespoons maple syrup

1 vanilla pod, split and seeds scraped (or ¼ teaspoon vanilla powder or extract)

1–2 tablespoons almond milk (if the mixture needs thinning)

Preheat the oven to 180°C. Line a baking tray with baking paper and place ½ cup of the oats in a small bowl, ready for rolling.

Combine the mashed banana, remaining 2 cups of oats, walnuts, sultanas, grated apple, maple syrup, vanilla, coconut oil, almond butter, cinnamon, nutmeg and salt in a large bowl. Mix well using your hands, then shape into 16 balls. Roll the balls in the oats and place on the baking tray, flattening them just a touch with your hands.

Reduce the oven temperature to 160°C and bake these little babies for 30 minutes, or until golden brown. Leave them to cool while you whip up the creamy filling (though if you're anything like me you'll want to have a little nibble while they're still hot).

For the filling, pop everything except the almond milk into the food processor and blitz until you have a nice, thick but spreadable consistency, adding the almond milk little by little only if the mixture is too thick to spread.

To put the cookie sandwiches together, grab a cooled cookie and spread your filling all over the base, then sandwich it together with another cookie and there you have it. Enjoy!

Makes 8

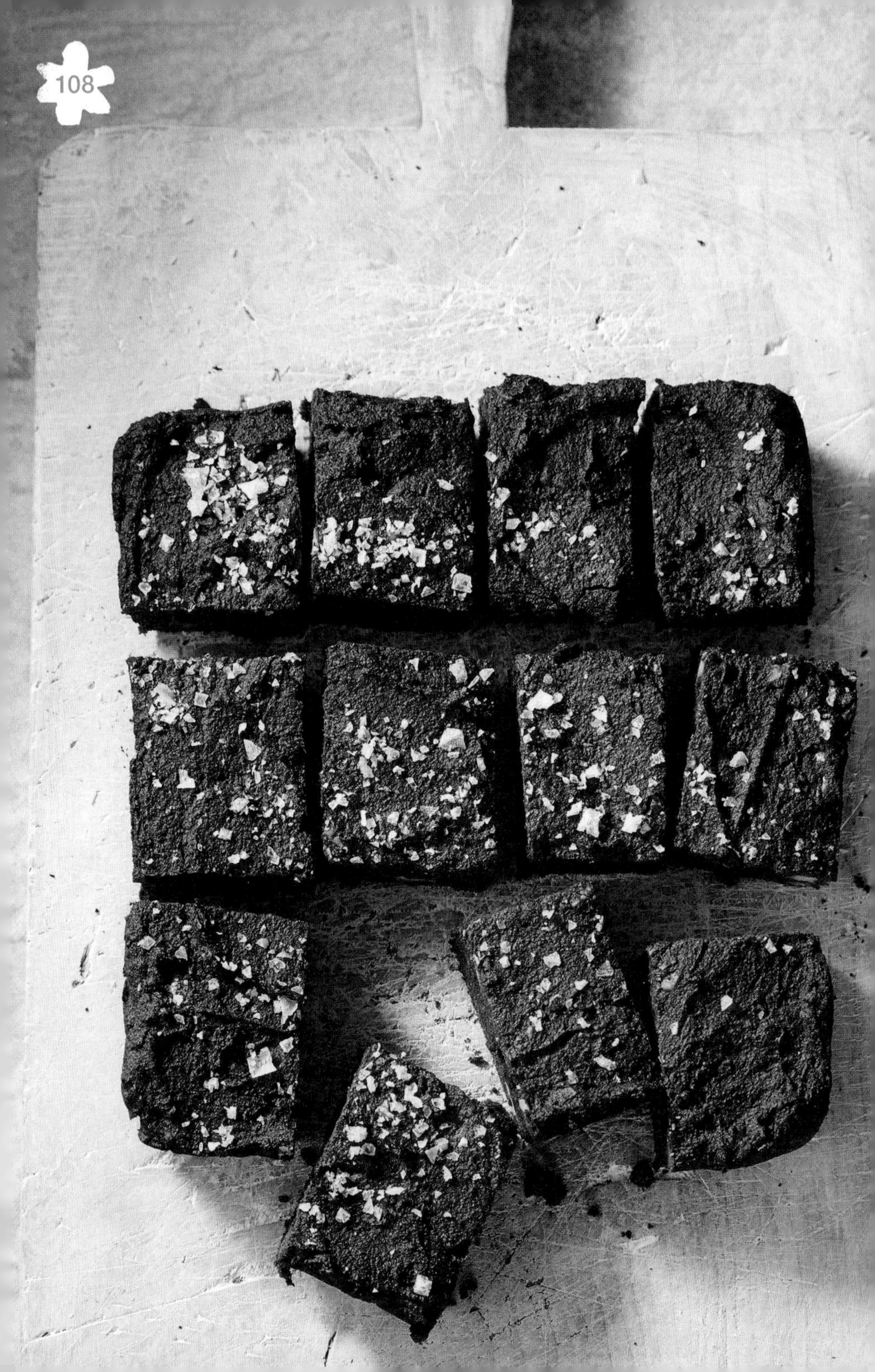

Avocado and walnut fudge brownies

✳

Before you say no to avocado in a sweet recipe, try this creation — it's so simple to make and the brownies have the best consistency ever. This recipe is full of good fats from the avo, coconut oil and walnuts, which make for the softest skin and silkiest hair, too. And it's also the perfect brain food!

¼ cup (60 ml) coconut oil, melted, plus extra for greasing

1 large avocado

1 cup (180 g) medjool dates, pitted

⅓ cup (80 ml) maple syrup

1 vanilla pod, split and seeds scraped (or ¼ teaspoon vanilla powder or extract)

salt flakes

3 large eggs, whisked

½ cup (55 g) almond meal

½ cup (55 g) coconut flour

⅓ cup (40 g) cacao powder

1 cup (125 g) roughly chopped walnuts

coconut ice cream, to serve (optional)

Preheat the oven to 180°C. Grease a 20 cm square baking tin with coconut oil.

Pop the avo, dates, maple syrup, coconut oil, vanilla and a pinch of salt into a food processor or blender and blitz everything together well. Spoon the mixture into a big bowl and stir through the eggs, then add the almond meal, coconut flour and cacao powder and mix together gently until well combined. Stir in the walnuts, then scoop the brownie mix into your baking tin using a spatula (it'll be pretty sticky). Sprinkle over a last pinch of salt and bake for 20 minutes, or until soft and fudgy.

Leave the brownies to cool for 10 minutes, then slice and serve with coconut ice cream for a really dreamy dessert, or just enjoy them on their own. The brownies will keep for up to 4 days in the fridge and can be kept frozen for much longer.

Makes 12

The perfect paleo parsnip cake

*

I know this sounds more like a savoury vegetable dish, but bear with me here; it's a lovely treat that not only feeds the skin but also encourages the whole body to thrive. Extra-virgin olive oil is a bit of an all-rounder and delivers many health benefits to the body, whether applied topically or eaten, like this. When consumed it's said to aid the digestive system, help to reduce our levels of bad cholesterol and even help lower blood pressure.

coconut oil, for greasing

3 cups (300 g) almond meal

1 teaspoon ground cinnamon

½ teaspoon ground nutmeg

pinch of salt flakes

½ teaspoon bicarbonate
of soda

5 large eggs

½ cup (125 ml) maple syrup
(or honey or coconut nectar)

2 tablespoons extra-virgin
olive oil

2 cups (210 g) grated parsnip

1 large granny smith apple,
grated

½ cup (60 g) sultanas

½ cup (60 g) raisins

½ cup (60 g) roughly chopped
walnuts, plus extra to serve

½ cup (60 g) roughly
chopped pecans,

Icing

2 cups (500 g) ricotta

½ cup (125 ml) maple syrup

1 vanilla pod, split and seeds
scraped (or ¼ teaspoon
vanilla powder or extract)

½ teaspoon ground cinnamon

Preheat the oven to 180°C. Lightly grease a 20 cm cake
tin with a little coconut oil and line the base with a circle
of baking paper.

Combine all the dry ingredients in a large bowl.
Make a little well in the centre and crack in the eggs,
then add the maple syrup and olive oil and mix together
really well to get rid of any lumps. Stir through the parsnip,
apple, sultanas, raisins, walnuts and pecans.

Spoon the batter into the prepared tin and smooth the
surface, then bake for 1 hour, or until a skewer inserted
into the centre of the cake comes out clean. Remove from
the oven and leave to cool.

While the cake is cooling, whip up the icing. The easiest
way is to mix the ingredients in a food processor or
blender, but you can do it by hand; you just want to make
sure everything's mixed evenly and there are no lumps.

Slather the icing over the top of the cooled cake,
then slice and serve.

Serves 8–10

HOMEMADE
SKIN
TREATMENTS

Mocha-licious body scrub

This scrub helps to minimise cellulite and stimulate circulation. I love the mocha aroma of chocolate and coffee, and if you add a few drops of orange essential oil it adds a whole new dimension (plus adding essential oils brings other health benefits). There are so many essential oils you can try instead of orange in this recipe. I also love adding lavender oil for a calming night-time scrub before bed. Peppermint, on the other hand, is invigorating and stimulating, so makes a great addition to a morning scrub!

⅓ cup (25 g) ground coffee

1 tablespoon cacao nibs

1 heaped teaspoon cacao powder

⅓ cup (60 g) brown sugar

½ cup (125 ml) extra-virgin olive oil

5 drops of orange essential oil

Mix the ingredients together thoroughly and store in a sealed glass jar until needed. To use, rub the scrub in a circular motion all over your body, or just into the problem areas. This works best on a wet body, so I jump in the shower and turn the water off while I exfoliate, then turn the water back on to rinse it off.

I store this scrub on the ledge in my bathroom. Handy tip, though: because it contains sugar the ants will love it, so make sure you keep it in some sort of sealed jar or container! This will make enough for three full body scrubs.

Turkish delight body butter

This little concoction helps moisturise and prevent skin ageing, and the cacao is full of antioxidants. It will keep for ages stored in a jar out of direct sunlight (I've had some of my creations for over a year). I use it most nights, to be honest, and multiple times a day in the summer to feed my skin if it's getting a tad more sun exposure.

½ cup (115 g) cocoa butter

½ cup (125 ml) coconut oil, melted

½ cup (125 ml) extra-virgin olive oil

1 heaped tablespoon cacao powder

10 drops of rose essential oil

Mix the ingredients together thoroughly and store in a sealed glass jar until needed. Use in place of your regular body moisturiser – it may be oilier than you're used to, so a little goes a long way. Give it time after towel-drying to soak in, too. Or, if you're worried about being super oily, then use it at night after towel-drying after a hot shower, so your pores are open – your skin should soak it up nicely. Then you will wake up with silky smooth skin!

TIP This is also lovely to use on your face.

Cheeky monkey body mask

This one is hard not to eat, it's so yummy! This scrub will keep for 3 days in the fridge, though without the bananas it would last up to a year, so you can always make up a big batch without bananas and then add them to the mix when needed.

2 ripe bananas

2 tablespoons cacao powder

½ cup (125 ml) coconut oil, melted

¼ cup (25 g) desiccated coconut

¼ cup (30 g) cacao nibs

Mix the ingredients together thoroughly. Give yourself a rinse in the shower, then turn the water off and scrub. It will be messy, but it will smell amazing and you'll feel great after. Rinse off. This will make enough for two whole body masks.

TIP Go for organic desiccated coconut without the preservatives here to make sure it's gentler on your skin.

FIVE

HAIR

RECIPES AND REMEDIES

Hero ingredients

I'm all about the mermaid hair, so I love doing treatments to get that smooth texture and shine. I also love being able to wear my hair out and flowy without doing too much to it. That said, this book is all about natural beauty and I want to be honest and up-front here: in the past I've had a little help with extensions and although I love having long locks, it isn't always my own hair. So, I decided for this book that I wanted it to be totally natural, which is why I have shorter hair that's all mine. I am all for doing whatever you want to do to make yourself feel your best, and if that means extensions then go for it, but these next recipes and remedies are all the things I do for my natural locks.

Coconut oil

I love using coconut oil in my hair – to the extent that I'll walk into a room and people will say, 'Oh wow! You smell of coconut oil!' To which I like to say, 'I'm going for tropical mermaid.' But you know what? I love it! I think we should all use it topically and in our diets for hair health. Coconut oil hair masks have been used to promote hair growth and we know that consuming it is a great way to promote healthy hair growth (see page 166).

Eggs

Eggs are another brilliant source of not just good fats but also complete proteins, so if you're a vegetarian, keeping eggs in your diet is key for hair health. The cool thing about eggs is that you can also use them topically in your hair. The yolk and whites do different things and will work differently depending on your hair type (they have even been used topically in folk medicine for soothing the skin, while beaten egg white was an old folk remedy for relieving bruises and sprains). On top of all this, they're also a great source of the vitamin biotin (or vitamin B7), which is needed for scalp health and hair growth.

Salmon

This is the one food where, if I include it in my diet, I really notice a difference when it comes to my hair. It's rich in omega 3 fatty acids, which we know are great for shiny and silky hair, and on top of that it's a complete protein. I'm sure you've heard of the protein 'keratin' – a special protein which is in charge of giving hair strength and flexibility – well, salmon is full of it, making it brilliant for long, luscious locks.

Best gluten-free banana bread

✦

I'm a banana bread fiend, so I'd like to think I'm a bit of an expert at the old gluten-free banana creation by now. This recipe contains two of our hair heroes: coconut oil and eggs. One of my favourite health writers, David Gillespie, describes eggs as the perfect superfood – they're pretty easy to digest and they're full of all the things we need, such as proteins, good fats and minerals like calcium, iron, potassium, magnesium and zinc, not to mention vitamins A, B complex, C, D, E and folic acid.

3 tablespoons coconut oil, melted, plus extra for greasing

1 cup (200 g) quinoa flour

½ cup (60 g) quinoa flakes

2 teaspoons gluten-free baking powder

½ teaspoon ground cinnamon

¼ teaspoon ground nutmeg

1 vanilla pod, split and seeds scraped (or ¼ teaspoon vanilla powder or extract)

½ cup (45 g) desiccated coconut

pinch of salt flakes

2 large super-ripe bananas, plus 1 banana, thinly sliced

3 large eggs, lightly beaten

3 tablespoons maple syrup

Preheat the oven to 180°C and grease a 23 cm loaf tin with a little coconut oil.

Place the quinoa flour, quinoa flakes, baking powder, spices, vanilla, desiccated coconut and salt in a bowl and mix together thoroughly.

In a smaller bowl, mash together the 2 ripe bananas, then stir through the eggs, coconut oil and maple syrup.

Make a well in the centre of the dry ingredients and pour in the banana mixture. Mix well, using a wooden spoon to smooth out any lumpy bits. (You can use an electric cake mixer if you like, but there's something soothing about using the old-school method.

Pour the batter into your loaf tin and arrange the banana slices in tight rows on top (they will shrink a little when cooked). Bake for 20–25 minutes, or until a skewer inserted in the centre of the loaf comes out clean. Leave to cool and then share it with someone you love – even if that someone is you!

Makes 1 loaf

Egg white omelette

✳

Now, I still use two yolks in this recipe, but if you want to make it just with egg whites then that's totally fine – it will still work a treat. I love using the yolks, though, because they are so rich in nutrients and good fats, which our hair, skin, bodies and minds thrive off. I'm an egg fiend and eat them most days – I love them cooked all different ways, too!

2 eggs

2 egg whites

¼ red onion, finely chopped

8 semi-sundried tomatoes

handful of baby spinach

½ cup (45 g) chopped Swiss or brown mushrooms

¼ cup (60 g) goat's feta, crumbled into small chunks

¼ bunch of basil, roughly chopped

salt flakes and freshly ground black pepper

1 teaspoon extra-virgin olive oil

1 avocado, sliced (optional)

micro herbs, such as mustard cress or radish cress, to serve (optional)

Crack the eggs and egg whites into a bowl and give them a quick, light whisk. Pop in the onion, tomatoes, spinach, mushrooms, feta and basil, give everything a quick whisk together and season with salt and pepper.

Heat the olive oil in a frying pan over a medium heat and pour in half of the omelette mix, then tilt the pan so it covers all of the base. Cook for 4 minutes, then carefully fold half the omelette over with a spatula so it looks like a half moon (take care as it's pretty chunky). Cook for another 2 minutes or so, then slide the omelette onto a plate and repeat with the rest of the mixture. Serve each omelette with a side of sliced avocado and some micro herbs, if you like. The perfect fast-food meal if you ask me!

Serves 2

TIPS
I like to leave the skin on the sweet potato for added nutritional value. I switch from fried to poached to boiled eggs like there's no tomorrow, so just cook the eggs here whatever way floats your boat.

Ultimate big brekkie

✲

The real heroes here are the sweet spud hash browns – they're so delicious,
and a pinch of cumin is the secret ingredient that makes all the difference!
They make a great side to almost any meal, especially steaks or simply cooked fish.
Try making up a big batch and freezing them for work or school lunches.

1 medium–large sweet potato,
washed and grated

¼ onion, diced

2 garlic cloves, diced

½ cup (55 g) almond meal

2 eggs

¼ teaspoon ground cumin

pinch of salt flakes and freshly
ground black pepper

1–2 tablespoons extra-virgin
olive oil or butter

To serve

2–4 eggs, cooked any way
you like

1 avocado, sliced into wedges

micro herbs, such as mustard
cress or radish cress, to serve

First, roll up the grated sweet spud in a clean tea towel
and squeeze to get as much of the liquid out as you can.
Tip it into a bowl with the onion, garlic, almond meal,
eggs, cumin and seasoning. Mix everything together well.

Heat the olive oil or butter in a frying pan over a medium
heat. Add the sweet spud mixture to the pan in ¼ cup
portions, using a spatula to flatten them. Cook the hash
browns for 3–5 minutes on each side, then serve them
up 2–3 per person with 1–2 eggs (any way you like),
a few slices of avocado and some micro herbs scattered
over the top.

Serves 2

Sweet potato wedges with egg, avo and basil

✤

This is a great way to create a really healthy meal without using refined grains. It is also very simple to whip up, and totally delicious!

1 sweet potato

1 tablespoon extra-virgin olive oil

1 avocado, cut into wedges

2 boiled eggs, peeled and finely grated

pinch of salt flakes and freshly ground black pepper

pinch of cayenne pepper

handful of basil leaves, to serve

Preheat the oven to 180°C and line a baking tray with baking paper.

Cut the sweet spud in half horizontally and then lengthways into 2 cm slices (the pieces should look like long boat shapes). Lay the sweet spud wedges out on the prepared tray in an even layer and drizzle over the olive oil, then bake for 20 minutes until softened.

Remove the wedges from the oven and divide between plates. Top with the avo wedges and grated egg, season with salt and pepper, sprinkle over the cayenne pepper and scatter over the basil leaves. Tuck in.

Serves 2

Salmon poke bowl

❋

Poke is all the rage at the moment and it's a really healthy and simple way to eat. This recipe works really well with sashimi-grade tuna or kingfish, too, and I have even used boiled eggs as the protein part with great results. I've seen people use tofu, too – I don't eat much tofu, but if you love it then give it a try. Remember, my number-one rule is to make healthy food work for you. That's the magic trick!

400 g sashimi-grade salmon, cut into 2 cm cubes

¼ cup (60 ml) gluten-free tamari

zest and juice of 1 lime

1 tablespoon sesame oil

1 cup (15 g) shredded red cabbage

1 avocado, diced

¼ red onion, thinly sliced

1 carrot, grated

3 radishes, finely sliced

1 zucchini, spiralised or grated

1 tablespoon sesame seeds, toasted

shredded nori, to serve

Pop the salmon in a bowl, then add the tamari, lime zest and juice and sesame oil. Set aside to marinate briefly while you assemble the salad.

Place the shredded cabbage on the bottom of four serving bowls like a little bed, then arrange the avocado, onion, carrot, radish and zucchini in pretty clusters on top. Tumble the salmon on top of the veg, spooning over the leftover marinade (which becomes a handy dressing for the salad), then scatter over the toasted sesame seeds. Serve topped with a little shredded nori.

Serves 4

TIPS
If you can't find shredded nori, just buy the sheets and finely slice.

My favourite crispy salmon and salad

＊

Salmon is one of my ultimate beauty foods — it's not just great for the hair, but is also good for the skin, nails … you name it. The good fats in the salmon will make your hair glossy and healthy. When I include lots of salmon and oily fish in my diet it shows in the glow of my skin and the shine in my locks!

4 x 180 g salmon fillets (skin on)

salt flakes and freshly ground black pepper

⅓ cup (80 ml) coconut oil

Salad

1 punnet (250 g) cherry tomatoes, halved

2 large handfuls of rocket, washed and dried

1 avocado, diced

¼ red onion, finely sliced

¼ bunch of fresh dill

12 green olives, pitted and sliced

½ cup (60 g) walnuts, roughly chopped

3 tablespoons extra-virgin olive oil

2 teaspoons apple cider vinegar

salt flakes and freshly ground black pepper

Heat a frying pan over a medium–high heat for 2 minutes. Season the salmon fillets with salt and pepper. Melt the coconut oil in the pan and immediately add the salmon, skin-side down, and cook for 3 minutes. Turn the salmon and cook for a further minute — the salmon should have a crispy skin and medium–rare flesh. Remove from the pan and set aside to rest.

Meanwhile, to make the salad, place the tomatoes, rocket, avocado, onion, dill, olives and walnuts in a salad bowl. Mix the olive oil and vinegar together in a separate small bowl to make a dressing, then pour it over the salad ingredients and give everything a good old mix about. Season the salad with salt and pepper and serve alongside the crispy salmon.

Serves 4

TIPS
Be sure to dry the rocket thoroughly after washing because otherwise it drains all the flavour from the salad dressing. If you want to keep the recipe low in fructose, just leave out the red onion.

Chicken burgers in lettuce cups

✱

This recipe is about as clean as it gets. Now, of course, you're the boss and you can most certainly serve these chicken burgers in buns if you like, but when I was in LA I noticed leafy greens like lettuce, collard greens, kale and English spinach being used in the place of bread. It seems like a pretty smart way to enjoy your favourite burger or sanga without missing out, I reckon!

3 tablespoons coconut oil

1 onion, diced

2 carrots, grated

2 celery stalks, diced

500 g chicken mince

½ teaspoon ground cumin

⅓ cup (35 g) almond meal

2 eggs, lightly beaten

salt flakes and freshly ground black pepper

8 butter lettuce cups

2 large tomatoes, sliced into rounds

2 avocados, sliced lengthways

1 grated raw beetroot

½ cup (100 g) sauerkraut (homemade or store-bought)

To serve

extra-virgin olive oil

sesame seeds

chilli flakes (optional)

Melt 2 tablespoons of the coconut oil in a frying pan over a medium heat. Sauté the onion, carrot and celery for 2–3 minutes, or until the vegetables are soft and the onion is golden. Transfer to a mixing bowl and allow to cool. Add the chicken mince, cumin, 2 tablespoons of the almond meal and the eggs and season to taste. Mix well, divide into 8 portions and shape each into a pattie. Transfer to a plate, cover and refrigerate for 2–3 hours.

When the patties are firm, remove from the fridge. Place the remaining almond meal in a shallow bowl. Roll each pattie in the almond meal, coating it evenly.

Heat the remaining coconut oil in a large frying pan over a medium heat. Place 3 patties in the pan and cook them for 5 minutes on each side, or until golden and cooked through. Keep warm and repeat with the remaining patties.

Place 2 lettuce cups on each plate. Line each cup with equal portions of the tomato rounds, avocado slices, grated beet and sauerkraut, then pop a pattie on top. To serve, drizzle with olive oil and sprinkle with sesame seeds and chilli flakes, if you like.

Serves 4

TIP
These patties
freeze really
well if you have
leftovers.

Gooey paleo cinnamon scrolls

✳

Righto, we're all friends here, so I want to say this – I don't make these too often at home because I love them so much I eat them all in one go. That's the truth! Now, I know this chapter is all about hair health – and we've got the coconut oil and egg heroes in here – but a quick word on how ace cinnamon is: it warms your whole system up, it helps to balance blood sugar and beat sugar cravings, it's said to help beat the common cold, externally it has been used as an antiseptic wash for wounds, in folk remedies it has been recommended as an aphrodisiac and it has even been more valuable than gold at times. So these cinnamon scrolls may become very special in your household!

2 cups (200 g) almond meal

½ cup (70 g) coconut flour, plus extra for sprinkling

pinch of salt flakes

⅓ cup (80 ml) maple syrup

2 large eggs, at room temperature

1 vanilla pod, split and seeds scraped (or ¼ teaspoon vanilla powder or extract)

¼ cup (30 g) chopped pecans

pinch of ground cinnamon

Filling

½ cup (125 ml) maple syrup

¼ cup (60 ml) coconut oil, melted

1 teaspoon ground cinnamon

¼ cup (30 g) raisins (or currants)

½ cup (60 g) chopped pecans

¼ teaspoon ground nutmeg

¼ cup (30 g) sultanas

½ cup (80 g) roughly chopped medjool dates

Glaze

¼ cup (60 ml) maple syrup

¼ cup (60 ml) coconut cream

2 tablespoons coconut oil, melted

Preheat the oven to 180°C and line a baking tray with baking paper.

Place the almond meal, coconut flour, salt, maple syrup, eggs and vanilla in a bowl and mix together to form a dough. If the dough needs thickening, just add a touch more coconut flour. Roll the dough into a ball, wrap in plastic wrap and pop it in the fridge for about 30 minutes to rest.

To make the filling, place all the ingredients in a small bowl and mix together well.

Once rested, take the dough out of the fridge, sprinkle it all over with coconut flour to prevent it from sticking, then put it between two sheets of baking paper and flatten. Cut the edges into a square shape (pressing any excess dough evenly back on top) and roll out to about 1 cm thick. Be gentle when rolling so the mixture doesn't crack. Remove the baking paper, spoon the filling over the top and spread it out evenly. (I leave 2–3 cm along one side so there is an edge to stick it together and so I don't overload the filling.) Roll the dough into a log shape, then slice the log into 4–5 cm segments. Lay the scrolls cut-side down on the baking tray and bake for 15 minutes, or until lightly golden. Remove from the oven and leave to cool.

When the scrolls are cool, mix the maple syrup, coconut cream and oil together to make a glaze and drizzle over the top (this is best done using a blender or electric mixer to get a nice smooth texture). Sprinkle over the pecans and cinnamon and enjoy. Good luck having just the one!

Makes 8–10

Magical macaroons

✳

These little treats are super good for your hair and tick all the paleo and vegan boxes. If you'd like to tailor them to make them fructose friendly then just replace the maple syrup with rice malt syrup. This recipe would also make an awesome body scrub — give it a try and your skin will be thanking you too!

½ cup (125 ml) coconut oil, melted, plus extra if necessary

½ cup (55 g) almond meal

3 tablespoons maple syrup, plus extra if necessary

1 cup (90 g) desiccated coconut

½ teaspoon ground nutmeg

1 vanilla pod, split and seeds scraped (or ¼ teaspoon vanilla powder or extract)

pinch of salt flakes

Combine all the ingredients in a large bowl and mix together thoroughly, adding a little more coconut oil and another tablespoon of maple syrup if the mixture is too crumbly. Shape the mixture into little balls (it's easier with damp hands), arrange them on a tray and whack them in the freezer for about 20 minutes to set. Store in an airtight container in the fridge for up to 2 weeks and share them with your mates.

Makes about 20

S'mores protein balls

✳

This is my favourite thing at the moment when I'm craving a treat – it really ticks all the boxes. Now, I know that marshmallows aren't uber healthy or vegan, so they are totally optional, but they do make these balls pretty darn amazing. Try to find chocolate chips that are naturally sweetened with stevia, or if you want to keep it vegan then use ½ cup of raw cacao nibs instead; they won't be quite as tasty, but they give good crunch. As with all of my recipes, tweak this to make it suit you and your tastebuds!

1 cup (100 g) rolled oats

⅔ cup (60 g) desiccated coconut, plus 1 cup (90 g) extra for rolling

½ cup (55 g) vanilla whey protein powder

2 tablespoons chia seeds

½ cup (25 g) puffed quinoa

½ cup (125 g) almond butter

⅓ cup (80 ml) maple syrup

½ cup (125 ml) coconut oil, melted

1 cup (170 g) chocolate chips

½ cup (45 g) gluten-free marshmallows, chopped into small chunks (optional)

Pop everything except the extra desiccated coconut for rolling into a big bowl and mix it together, or put the lot in your food processor and give it a good blitz. Divide the mixture into 12 even-sized pieces and roll them out into balls with wet hands (this will help prevent the mixture sticking to your hands).

Spread the remaining desiccated coconut out evenly over a baking tray. Add the balls to the coconut and roll to cover evenly, then store in the fridge for about half an hour to set. Eat straight from the fridge (where they will keep for up to 3 weeks in an airtight container).

Makes 12

HOMEMADE
HAIR
TREATMENTS

Luscious lavender oil treatment

This hair treatment is the one I always come back to – it's a goodie, and if I do it at night it always calms me down before bed. You can swap lavender for rosemary oil if you want to help stimulate hair growth, but one day I went too hard on the rosemary oil and I smelled like a Sunday roast for a week afterwards!

¼ cup (60 ml) coconut oil, melted

2 tablespoons olive oil

8 drops of lavender essential oil

All you have to do is combine the oils (making sure the coconut oil is melted first, otherwise it makes things really tricky to combine). Keep it in a little jar in your bathroom cabinet, applying it to your mid-lengths and ends as needed. Wash twice with shampoo afterwards before conditioning as usual.

TIPS Try to use regular olive oil here rather than extra-virgin, unless you don't mind it smelling quite olive oily. I have made the mistake of putting this on my roots, too, and the oils just don't come out of the roots very well, so stick to mid-lengths and ends for best results.

Moisturising avocado hair mask

Righto, so this one is super simple and it's great because it can penetrate the surface of the hair. This combo might sound weird, but we're using it like a mask, so you pop it on wet hair and then leave it for 10–15 minutes before shampooing and conditioning as usual. This mixture will keep in the fridge for about a week.

¼ cup (60 ml) avocado oil

2 tablespoons raw honey

¼ cup (35 g) plain unsweetened yoghurt

Mix everything together well in a bowl. Now, often with hair masks they say to shampoo, then do the treatment, then condition, but I love to just wet my hair and then pop this in for about 10–15 minutes. (I'll often stay in the shower and exfoliate my body while it works its magic.)

Then, before I wet my hair again I pop the shampoo in and start to lather it up – the shampoo will help to stop the oil sticking to your hair. (When I go straight for water before the shampoo this can get a bit sticky, because the water and oil don't like each other, but this way round the oil lifts off easy-peasy, making it the go for any oily treatment). Then I rinse, shampoo and condition as normal! The avocado oil helps to keep my hair feeling shiny and strong. This will keep for 2–3 days in the fridge.

Super simple egg treatment

This is so, so simple! And it works wonders, though if you have super-oily hair this might not be your thing (my hair is naturally really dry so it loves this treatment). If you do have oily hair, follow the recipe but just use two egg whites and no yolks. Eggs have been used for yonks in homemade hair treatments to both strengthen the hair (thanks to the protein and lecithin content) and make it silky and smooth (thanks to the natural fats).

2 eggs

¼ cup (60 ml) extra-virgin olive oil

Just mix the eggs and oil together, then apply this mixture to your mid-lengths and ends (I keep it off my roots because oils are just that little bit harder to get out). Then tie your hair up into a messy bun, watch a bit of TV or do some emails for 20–30 minutes (or up to 2 hours, if you like) then shampoo it out twice before conditioning as usual. When you dry your hair you should notice it feels silky, smooth, luscious and strong! This will make enough for four treatments. Store it in the fridge.

TIP I use this quantity of eggs and olive oil, but I also have loads of thick hair, so if that's not you, I'm sure you could use half the amount and still get brilliant results!

SIX

NAILS

RECIPES AND REMEDIES

Hero ingredients

I find there's something really feminine about having nice healthy-looking nails.
I know that might sound a bit princess-like, but I do feel my best when I've been
looking after my nails and hands. I always notice my nails in meetings for some
reason, so I carry nail cream with me, and I'm always conscious of eating foods
that help with nail strength and growth.

Celery

Celery is one of the best food sources
of the mineral silica – one of the most
abundant elements on the planet. Yes, silica
is considered the 'beauty mineral'. We have
an abundance of it when we're younger, but
as we age we lose it. It's a mineral that's not
to be underestimated, as we need it for so
many other things. It's used by every single
cell and internal gland in our bodies. On top
of that, it has an impact on strengthening
the CVS (cardiovascular system) and the
nervous system, which needs calcium
and magnesium for transmission of nerve
impulses. It's also believed that silica may be
of value to the elderly for protection against
Alzheimer's, as it counteracts aluminium's
effects on the body by aiding its removal
(see page 166). So, it's fair to say that this is
probably one of my favourite minerals and
I don't really go a day without eating celery.

Oysters

Oysters are one of the best food sources
of zinc, which we need for loads of functions
in the body. Zinc is key for tissue growth
and that includes our hair, skin and nails.
It also helps with healing, so if you ever get
little nicks and scratches around your nails,
this is something zinc will help with.

Paprika

What a spice! Paprika is packed full of
vitamins B, C and E, as well as iron, which
makes it the perfect nail spice. Its awesome
colour comes from the carotenoids (beta-
carotene) which are brilliant for not just
nail health but skin health as well, and are
said to be a preventative when it comes
to ageing skin and sun damage. Plus, this
ace spice has anti-inflammatory properties.
You know when your nail beds get red
sometimes? This happens to me when
there's inflammation in my body, often from
eating something I shouldn't have, such as
gluten, dairy or refined sugars. By upping
this lovely red spice, I know I can help to
combat inflammation not only in my nail
beds but all over my body.

The ultimate detox juice

Juicing is a great way to get added nutrition in. To be clear, I'm not a massive fan of gruelling detox fasts, but I love including a juice like this in my daily eating plan, especially if I know I've been overindulging. It's a great way to get you feeling tiptop again. And while it's full of minerals that are great for your nails, your whole body will love you for this creation. It's also fructose free, vegan and paleo, so most people should be able to enjoy this one.

4 celery stalks

2 cucumbers

½ head of cos lettuce

2 bunches of baby spinach
(or 1 punnet)

1 lime

Pop everything through your juicer, divide between glasses or bottles and sip to your heart's content.

Serves 2

TIP
Keep the skin on the
lime if your juicer can
handle it, as it contains
heaps of health benefits.
Lemons work great in
the place of limes, too.

Healthy bloody Mary

* ~~~~~~~~~~~~~~~~~~~~~~

This recipe can be non-alcoholic if you prefer, but I will definitely give you the option to make it alcoholic – after all, life's about balance right? There's just something I love about tomato juice, which is why I think I could drink it every day! The addition of raw garlic makes it pretty potent and a huge immunity booster.

5 large, round tomatoes
(truss work well, too)

6 celery stalks, plus a few baby
celery leaves to serve

1 garlic clove

2 limes

pinch of cayenne pepper,
plus extra to serve

pinch of salt flakes,
plus extra to serve

dash of Worcestershire sauce,
plus extra to serve

dash of Tabasco, plus extra
to serve

2 shots vodka (optional)

ice cubes

freshly ground black pepper

Put your tomatoes, celery, garlic and limes through a juicer into a jug. Add the cayenne pepper, salt, Worcestershire sauce, Tabasco and vodka, if using, and mix well.

Fill two glasses with a generous amount of ice, then pour over the bloody Mary mix. Season each glass with an extra pinch each of cayenne pepper and salt and a dash each of Worcestershire sauce and Tabasco. Stir, then finish each glass with a few baby celery leaves and a crack of black pepper. Serve.

Serves 2

Zucchini chips
with raw vegan aioli

✿

These are great for people who crave salty things like potato chips, as they're a way healthier option. I'm a big believer that when you pull something out of your diet, you should replace it with a healthier version so you don't feel like you're missing out.

1 zucchini

salt flakes and freshly ground black pepper

2 tablespoons extra-virgin olive oil

2 garlic cloves, crushed (optional)

pinch of smoked paprika

pinch of chilli flakes

Aioli

½ cup (80 g) cashews

zest and juice of 1 lime

2 garlic cloves, crushed

¼ red chilli, finely sliced (use more if you like)

½ teaspoon salt flakes

pinch of paprika or dried chilli flakes

Slice the zucchini into very thin discs using a knife or mandoline. Sprinkle with salt then place them on paper towel and let them sweat for 1 hour.

Preheat the oven to 160°C and line a baking tray with baking paper.

Pat the zucchini discs dry with paper towel to remove the excess salt and moisture, then place them on the baking tray. Drizzle with the olive oil, scatter over the garlic, if using, sprinkle over the spices and season with salt and pepper. Bake for 30 minutes – the chippies will be crispy and delish when they're ready!

For the aioli, place the cashews, lime zest and juice, garlic, chilli and salt in a blender with ¼ cup (60 ml) of water and blend until thick and creamy. Spoon into a bowl and sprinkle over the paprika or chilli flakes.

Use your zucchini chippies as dippers and enjoy!

Serves 2

Oysters three ways

✻

Oysters are one of the best food sources of zinc, which we need for so many functions in the body, but zinc is also a key player when it comes to skin, hair and nail health. Here are some simple ways to jazz them up.

24 oysters

Natural

lemon wedges, to serve

Chilli and lime

zest and juice of 1 lime

⅓ cup (80 ml) apple cider vinegar

2 tablespoons extra-virgin olive oil

1 tablespoon coconut sugar

1 chilli, finely chopped (remove the pith and seeds if you don't want it too hot)

6 coriander leaves, finely sliced

Vinaigrette

2 tablespoons white wine vinegar

2 tablespoons red wine vinegar

1 spring onion, very finely sliced

pinch of salt flakes

For natural, just serve the oysters with a few wedges of fresh lemon (this is actually my favourite way to eat oysters, especially when they're super fresh).

For the chilli and lime combo, all you have to do is mix the ingredients together in a small bowl until the sugar dissolves, then serve them with a teaspoon so you can spoon the dressing over the top of each oyster before eating. The same goes for the vinaigrette – mix everything together well in a bowl, then use a teaspoon to drizzle the dressing over the oyster before slurping it down!

Serves 2

Celery and apple slaw

One of my dad's favourite savoury dishes is coleslaw, so this one is for him – and it's a much healthier version than the store-bought ones out there. It's easy to make and has a few twists to make it different. Take this along to a barbecue or party and it might just steal the show!

8 celery stalks, sliced into little half moons, baby leaves reserved to serve

2 large granny smith apples, cut into thin wedges

½ cup (50 g) walnut halves

½ cup (65 g) dried cranberries

salt flakes and freshly ground black pepper

zest and juice of 1 lemon

1 tablespoon dijon mustard

2 tablespoons honey

3 tablespoons extra-virgin olive oil

Grab a glass serving bowl and pop in your celery moons, apple wedges, walnuts and cranberries. Season with salt and pepper.

In a separate small bowl, mix the lemon zest and juice together with the mustard, honey and olive oil to make a dressing. Pour the dressing over the salad and toss together well, then top with a few baby celery leaves. Eat straight away.

Serves 4 as a side

TIP
You can always use
dried chickpeas here
instead of canned – simply
soak them overnight
before cooking as above.

Paprika baked falafel with hummus

✤

I love falafel, but sometimes it can be hard to find gluten-free ones that don't upset my tummy. These ones are mega healthy and they're baked not fried, which makes them extra clean. Rinsing the chickpeas twice helps to remove the phytic acid, which means you'll be less likely to feel bloated after eating them. You can add these to a salad, have them as a snack or serve them up just like this with a fresh hummus dip!

Falafel

1 x 400 g can chickpeas, rinsed twice

2 spring onions, chopped

1 heaped teaspoon smoked paprika

2 tablespoons almond meal

½ cup (125 g) tomato paste

juice of 1 lemon

salt flakes and freshly ground black pepper

2 tablespoons extra-virgin olive oil

Hummus

1 x 400 g can chickpeas, rinsed twice

2 tablespoons tahini

½ cup (125 ml) extra-virgin olive oil

zest and juice of 1 lemon

4 cherry tomatoes

salt flakes and freshly ground black pepper

large pinch of smoked paprika

Preheat the oven to 180°C and line a baking tray with baking paper.

Place all the falafel ingredients in a food processor and whiz together to combine. Using wet hands, roll the mixture out into 8–10 golf ball–sized balls, then arrange them on the baking tray in an even layer and press them down so they're oval shaped. Bake for 15 minutes or until golden, then flip over and bake for a further 5 minutes.

While the falafel are baking, make the hummus. Pop the chickpeas in the food processor together with the tahini, oil, lemon zest and juice and cherry tomatoes and whiz them up until you've got a nice paste. Season with salt and pepper. Use a spatula to scoop the mixture into a bowl, then sprinkle over the paprika.

To serve, remove the baked falafel from the oven and leave them to cool a tad, then dip them into the hummus while still warm. Just try to stop yourself eating the whole lot – they're that good!

Serves 2

Collard green wraps

✱

I discovered these genius creations in LA. Essentially, we're using a collard green leaf in the place of a bread wrap. You can use any strong leafy green, such as silverbeet, kale, English spinach or rainbow chard – whatever you can get your hands on (and if your leaves aren't that sturdy, double the number and layer one on top of the other to make them strong enough to hold the filling). Now this filling is raw and vegan, but you can totally add any protein you like – I like adding spicy chicken to the mix sometimes.

4 large collard green leaves
(or silverbeet, kale, English
spinach or rainbow chard)

1 avocado, sliced

8 semi-sundried tomatoes,
roughly chopped

½ cup (45 g) mung bean
sprouts

1 carrot, grated

1 zucchini, grated

1 punnet (125 g) blueberries

½ cup (80 g) macadamia nuts,
roughly chopped

⅓ cup (80 g) almond butter

salt flakes and freshly ground
black pepper

pinch of chilli flakes (optional)

Grab the first leaf and arrange a layer of avocado slices down the middle in a rough line. Top with a few semi-sundried tomatoes, a scattering of mung beans, some carrot, zucchini, blueberries and a quarter of the chopped macas. Down one side, spread 1 tablespoon of almond butter, season and add the chilli flakes (if using). Then tightly wrap up your pressie – I fold the 'bottom' edge first, then bring both the longer sides in, a bit like a Mexican tortilla wrap. Repeat with the remaining wraps and serve.

Serves 4

Super soup

*

I love making soup because it's a great way to sneak in so many health benefits.
This one not only boosts your hair, skin and nails, it also has a thermogenic effect on
the body and is a great way to help speed up your metabolism! I love it because it's so
easy to make in a big batch and freeze for a healthy no-fuss lunch or dinner.
Also, if you want to make this creation vegan, hold the pecorino and replace it
with a nice nut cheese instead.

1 tablespoon extra-virgin olive oil

2 garlic cloves, diced

1 onion, diced

1 red chilli, finely chopped

1 teaspoon paprika (smoked or sweet), plus extra to serve

½ bunch celery, stalks diced, tops roughly chopped

2 cups (400 g) chopped tomatoes

2 carrots, roughly chopped

1 cup (155 g) diced sweet potato

½ head of cauliflower, cut into small chunks

¼ head of green cabbage, finely sliced or shredded

1 cup (200 g) quinoa (any colour or type – I love the tri-coloured)

salt flakes and freshly ground black pepper

2 large handfuls of baby spinach

handful of basil leaves, torn

¼ cup (25 g) grated pecorino cheese, to serve

large handful of cherry tomatoes, to serve (optional)

Heat the olive oil in a large, heavy-based saucepan over a medium–high heat. Add the garlic, onion, chilli and paprika and sauté for 1 minute, then add the diced celery stalks and cook a further 2 minutes. Add the chopped tomatoes, carrot, sweet potato and 1.5 litres of water and bring to the boil, then reduce the heat and simmer for 20 minutes.

Add the cauliflower, cabbage and quinoa and cook for a further 5–10 minutes (or 10–15 if you prefer less crunchy quinoa). Season to taste, add the celery tops and spinach and immediately remove from heat. Serve with torn basil, a sprinkling of paprika, a generous scattering of grated pecorino and a couple of cherry tomatoes, if you like.

Serves 6

TIP
If you don't have any fresh tomatoes, use a can of whole peeled tomatoes and chop them up.

Veggo curry with quinoa

❋

This recipe was my go-to when I was vegan – I'd mix it up with whatever veggies I had on hand and what was most seasonal. Personally, I love having a few meat-free days, and this recipe is full of fibre and protein so it is guaranteed to leave you feeling full afterwards. I've also made it with other beans and legumes in the place of chickpeas and it works a treat, so have a play and make your very own version of this veggo curry!

2 tablespoons extra-virgin olive oil

1 onion, diced

2 garlic cloves, finely diced

2 stalks celery, sliced

1 tablespoon grated ginger

2 x 400 g cans chickpeas, rinsed twice

2 cups (about 240 g) cubed pumpkin

2 cups (about 280 g) cubed sweet potato

1 zucchini, roughly chopped

¼ teaspoon ground turmeric

½ teaspoon ground cumin

½ teaspoon ground coriander

½ teaspoon paprika

1 teaspoon mustard seeds

2 x 400 ml cans coconut cream

salt flakes and freshly ground black pepper

2 tablespoons desiccated coconut

½ teaspoon coriander seeds

2 cups (400 g) tri-coloured quinoa, rinsed

1 cup (150 g) cashews

2 cups (60 g) roughly chopped coriander leaves

juice of 1 lime

Heat the olive oil in a large frying pan over a medium heat. Add the onion and sauté for 2 minutes, or until translucent. Add the garlic, celery and ginger and sauté for another minute, then pop in the chickpeas, pumpkin, sweet spud, zucchini, spices, one can of the coconut cream and 3 cups (750 ml) of water. Season with salt and pepper and simmer over a low heat for 30 minutes.

Meanwhile, place the remaining can of coconut cream in another saucepan along with the desiccated coconut, coriander seeds and quinoa and 1–2 cups (250–500 ml) of water to cover. Bring to the boil, then reduce the heat, cover and simmer for 15 minutes, or until you notice the quinoa has grown to about three times its size. Set aside and keep warm.

When the pumpkin and sweet spud are nice and soft, add the cashews and stir them through. Serve the curry over the coconut quinoa and top with the coriander leaves and a good squeeze of fresh lime.

Serves 4

Pretty awesome
paleo shepherd's pie

✱

This is the perfect healthy alternative to something that can often be a bit of a treat. In fact, I reckon it tastes even better than the real thing! Yes, it contains two of our hero foods, but I also want to quickly mention onion, as we use it here and it's a bit of an unsung hero. Over the years, onion has been used in folk remedies to treat gout, digestive problems and even to help prevent the common cold, while in ancient Egypt it was believed to be a cure-all and a symbol of vitality.

⅓ cup (80 ml) extra-virgin olive oil

1 onion, diced

1 zucchini, grated

1 carrot, grated

2 celery stalks, finely chopped

½ teaspoon paprika

½ teaspoon ground cumin

salt flakes and freshly ground black pepper

500 g beef mince

1 cup (250 ml) chicken stock

1 head of cauliflower, roughly chopped

2 tablespoons butter

Preheat the oven to 180°C.

Heat half the olive oil in a large frying pan, add the onion and sauté for 2 minutes, or until translucent. Add the zucchini, carrot, celery and spices and cook for another minute. Season to taste, then add the beef and cook for 1–2 minutes, or until slightly browned. Pour in the chicken stock and simmer for 5–10 minutes, or until reduced to a thick, stewy consistency.

Meanwhile, place the cauliflower in a colander over a saucepan of boiling water and steam until just tender. Blitz in the food processor with the butter and a pinch of salt until smooth and creamy.

Pour the beef mixture into the base of an ovenproof baking dish. Top with the cauliflower mash and bake for 30 minutes. Remove from the oven, allow to cool and then dig in!

Serves 6

HOMEMADE NAIL TREATMENTS

Lemon and coconut nail oil

I love rubbing this into my nail beds, as I find it helps to prevent those little wispy bits of skin. I used to get them a fair bit and now I don't get them at all, which I put entirely down to this little gem of a creation. Stored in a sealed jar in the fridge, it will keep for yonks.

3 tablespoons coconut oil, melted

3 tablespoons extra-virgin olive oil

3 tablespoons macadamia oil

6 drops of lemon essential oil

Mix the ingredients together thoroughly and store in little containers in the fridge until needed. Rub a little of the oil into your nail beds and quicks to keep them healthy and strong, then pat off with a towel.

TIP If you want to mix this up a bit, try switching the lemon essential oil for another citrus essential oil – orange is lovely, too.

Oranges 'n honey cuticle rub

I love using nail cuticle rubs – they really help to look after my nail beds. And this might sound weird, but I also find that I seem to get longer out of any kind of nail polish or manicure if I'm looking after my cuticles. This one smells great!

50 g beeswax

2 tablespoons honey

¼ cup (60 ml) almond oil

6 drops of orange essential oil

Pop the beeswax in a little bowl and heat it over a small saucepan of boiling water on the stove until melted (alternatively, pop it in the microwave for a few seconds). Add the honey and mix it through, then mix in the almond oil and orange drops and stir until translucent. Pour into a little jar or container and keep it in the bathroom cabinet away from sunlight (it should last for a month or so). Rub a little into the nail beds and cuticles as needed.

Soak the saucepan and utensils in hot water afterwards to remove the wax.

TIP Beeswax can be found in health-food stores and some craft stores.

Raw sugar hand and nail scrub

This scrub keeps your nails and cuticles looking and feeling fresh and soft. To tell the truth, I end up using it all over my hands and it can even double as a lovely lip scrub and plumper. Keep it in a jar in the bathroom and use it whenever you can.

¼ cup (55 g) raw sugar

¼ cup (60 ml) extra-virgin olive oil

juice of 1 lemon (hold on to the lemon after you've juiced it, see Tip)

Righto, so just grab a bowl, mix the sugar, olive oil and lemon juice together, then store the scrub in a glass jar. I try to use this little creation up over the course of a week or so – it's a lovely full hand scrub and sometimes, if I'm at the end of a batch, I'll use it on my feet, too! Store in the fridge and shake before use.

TIP My mum taught me this one – rubbing your nails with the juiced lemon halves is brilliant for your cuticles. You can even rub them on your elbows to help prevent dry skin (now I'm giving away all your tricks, Mum!).

Notes

✸

CHAPTER 2: EYES

Page 65: The humble prune ... contains double the amount of antioxidants found in blueberries on the Oxygen Radical Absorbance Capacity (ORAC) scale: G. Cao, S. L. Booth, J. A. Sadowski, R. L. Prior, 'Increases in human plasma antioxidant capacity after consumption of controlled diets high in fruit and vegetables', *The American Journal of Clinical Nutrition*, vol. 68, no. 5, Nov. 1998, pp.1081–1087, ajcn.nutrition.org/content/68/5/1081.short

CHAPTER 3: SKIN

Page 90: [The body] absorbs around 65 per cent of what you put on it topically: H.S. Brown, D. R. Bishop, C. A. Rowan, 'The role of skin absorption as a route of exposure for volatile organic compounds (VOCs) in drinking water', *The American Journal of Public Health*, vol. 74, no. 5, November 1984, pp.479–484, ajph.aphapublications.org/doi/abs/10.2105/AJPH.74.5.479

CHAPTER 4: HAIR

Page 116: Consuming [coconut oil] is a great way to promote healthy hair growth: C. Muthu, M. Ayyanar, N. Raja, S. Ignacimuthu, 'Medicinal plants used by traditional healers in Kancheepuram District of Tamil Nadu, India', *Journal of Ethnobiology and Ethnomedicine*, vol. 2, no. 43, October 2006, ethnobiomed.biomedcentral.com/articles/10.1186/1746-4269-2-43

CHAPTER 5: NAILS

Page 142: It's also believed that silica may be of value to the elderly for protection against Alzheimer's, as it counteracts aluminium's effects on the body by aiding its removal: V. Rondeau, H. Jacqmin-Gadda, D. Commenges, C. Helmer, J-F. Dartigues, 'Aluminum and silica in drinking water and the risk of Alzheimer's disease or cognitive decline', *American Journal of Epidemiology 2008*, vol. 4, no.169, December 2008, pp.489–496, doi.org/10.1093/aje/kwn348

Thanks

✦

- First of all, I'd like to thank you; all of the people who support me, whether it be on Instagram, YouTube or Facebook, you are the people who go out and buy the books and inspire me to create more, so ultimately this book is as much yours as it is mine. It's all thanks to you!

- Mary Small, you were the first one to give me a go and believe in these creations. I'll be forever grateful.

- Clare Marshall, for bringing this dream to life and for believing in me and my quirky new idea.

- Ingrid Ohlsson, for always being so open to this exciting new concept!

- Armelle Habib, you are one photographer I could work with over and over again. I know you have my back and it's the best place to make magic from.

- Lauren Miller Cilento, we've built a sweet little team now. Feels like the dreams are coming true.

- Karina Duncan, growing with you makes me very happy. I love that you are part of these books.

- Michelle Mackintosh, you are a very magical human. I love seeing your visions come to life.

- Emma Warren. Guapa, you make me smile heaps. Keep loving from that awesome heart of yours!

- Emma Roocke, the queen of the perfect ball … Dare I say it, these ones were your best work yet!

- Simon Davis, thank you for making this book the best it can be!

- Steph Rooney, as always, I love working with you.

- Kate Radford, thanks for working your magic at the cover shoot. Such a treat to be in your presence.

- Tim O'Keefe, you're a keeper. It's always a dream to work with you and your brill music taste.

- Dominique Wrighton. Dommy, my green room bud, thank you for all your time and support.

- Hayley Van Spanje, you're a brilliant egg, and it means so much that you have my back.

- Emelia Wall, for your advice and constant fitspo!

- Leonie (Lee Lee) Sutherland, thank you for being a huge part of this journey.

- Lucy Roach, you were the first person to take a risk on me, and I'm always grateful.

- Charlotte Ree, thank you for spreading the word and helping these books shine.

- Linda Raymond. Lindi-Lou, my soul bud, you have my back and I have yours, forever.

- Dadio, thank you for always being my number-one supporter and for encouraging me to kick goals.
- Mum, your support is unwavering and so special.
- Andrea Evans (A. Apple), you're one of the most selfless people I know and I know we've got each other's backs forever!
- Maddie Dixson, my nature soul bud. Always listen to that heart of yours and trust it.
- Tristan Smith. Baby bro, you inspire me.
- Salvatore Malatesta. Sal, thank you for giving Happy Place wings, and for your passionate drive in business – it's very inspiring.
- Lach Ward, you live your passion a gentle way, and that is something I admire.
- Tayte Bale, I love working with you. You have a very sweet soul.
- Happy Place dream team. Bannie and the girls, thanks for making the magic and always trying new ideas. So nice to see that dream come to life.
- Rivis Donnelly, visiting you at Dymocks Melbourne is always a highlight for me. You care so much about what you do.
- Matt McMahon, you are a genius with a kind and very big heart.
- Rebecca Rich, thank you so much for being such a great recipe tester, with honest feedback.
- Nick Manuell, thank you for always looking after me.
- Leisel Jones. Chicken, you inspire me bucket-loads. You're real and honest, always stay that way!
- Faustina Agolley, thanks for always being so generous with your advice and time. It's been so awesome to watch you grow, keep shining!
- Dan Adair, for inspiring me to be the best version of myself.
- Reece Carter, thanks for being a great mate. More tea dates, please!
- Charlie Goldsmith, you are one inspiring bud. I'm very lucky to have you in my life, CG.
- Jamie Gonzalez, you show up to every book launch and every opening, and I am so grateful for that. Infinite bud!
- Bassike, Organic Crew and Tigerlily, so dreamy wearing your creations. Thank you.
- Yoke Yoga and Power Living, I travel all over the place and having both of your studios as bases is a huge help. It further helps my yoga to grow and develop, so I'm really grateful for that.

INDEX

A Plum book
First published in 2017 by
Pan Macmillan Australia Pty Limited
Level 25, 1 Market Street,
Sydney, NSW 2000, Australia

Level 3, 112 Wellington Parade,
East Melbourne, VIC 3002, Australia

Design by Michelle Mackintosh
Edited by Simon Davis
Index by Helena Holmgren
Photography by Armelle Habib
Prop and food styling by Karina Duncan
Food preparation by Emma Roocke and
    Emma Warren
Typeset by Pauline Haas
Colour reproduction by Splitting Image
    Colour Studio
Printed and bound in China by 1010 Printing
    International Limited

A CIP catalogue record for this book is available
from the National Library of Australia.

The publisher would like to thank the following
for their generosity in providing clothing for the
book: Bassike, Organic Crew and Tigerlily.

10 9 8 7 6 5 4 3 2 1